SNOOP DOGG PRESENTS

Goon
with the
Spoon

SNOOP DOGG

PRESENTS

Goon
with the
Spoon

**BY SNOOP DOGG AND
EARL "E-40" STEVENS**

CHRONICLE BOOKS
SAN FRANCISCO

FOREWORD

By SNOOP DOGG

E-40 is my big homie, my brother, my mentor. He paved the way for me on the West Coast.

In the 1990s, he was the first artist to show me the brand game and introduced me to the liquor business and St. Ides.

Watching him expand his love for food and cooking over the years to his many successful businesses is some boss-level shit. Which is why *Snoop Dogg Presents Goon with the Spoon* had to be the next cookbook, ya dig?

👊👨🏿‍🍳🔥🍽️

CHAPTER 1

BREAKFAST

Mimosas 3 Ways [15]

Morning-After Bloody Bar [17]

Roll It Up 'Rito [20]

Wake-and-Bake Meat Omelet [23]

Fried Chicken and
French Toast Sandwiches [26]

Corned Beef with All the Hash [30]

Mochi Muffins with
Pineapple and Coconut [33]

'Naner Bread [36]

Mimosas 3 Ways

SNOOP

Me and my guy E are triple threats, so we figured—why can't mimosas be that way too? Ain't nobody trippin' on a classic mimosa. What's there not to like?! Champagne mixed with ice-cold OJ sounds like a winner to me! But you know the boys gotta add a little kick in the mix. Move OJ to the side, ladies and gents, and elevate ya game with guava, blackberry lemonade, and pineapple-strawberry. Now you're playin' with the big DOGGS.

EACH MAKES 1 DRINK

GUAVA MIMOSA

4 oz [120 ml] champagne

2 oz [60 ml] guava juice

Lime slices, for garnish

Mint sprig, for garnish (optional)

1. Chill a champagne flute. Pour the champagne into the flute.

2. Top with the guava juice. Garnish with the lime slices and mint, if using. Serve immediately.

BLACKBERRY-LEMONADE MIMOSA

3 oz [90 ml] champagne

4 or 5 blackberries

3 oz [90 ml] lemonade

Lemon slice, for garnish

1. Chill a champagne flute. Pour the champagne into the flute.

2. Place 3 or 4 blackberries in a cocktail shaker and muddle until their juices are released, then add the lemonade. Cover the shaker and shake well for 30 seconds.

3. Strain into the champagne flute. Garnish with the lemon slice and a blackberry. Serve immediately.

PINEAPPLE-STRAWBERRY MIMOSA

3 oz [90 ml] champagne

3 strawberries, quartered, plus 1 for garnish

3 oz [90 ml] pineapple juice

Small pineapple wedge, for garnish

1. Chill a champagne flute. Pour the champagne into the flute.

2. Place the quartered strawberries in a cocktail shaker and muddle until their juices are released, then add the pineapple juice. Cover the shaker and shake well for 30 seconds.

3. Strain into the champagne flute. Garnish with the remaining strawberry and the pineapple wedge. Serve immediately.

Morning-After Bloody Bar

E-40 + SNOOP

✦ Us rappers have had some nights out, ya heard? Out here in Cali, we keep the good music, good vibes, and good dranks going well into the night. So the morning after, you've gotta reset with that iconic combo of tomato juice and vodka. Our Morning-After Bloody Bar kicks the flavors of your typical Bloody Mary up a notch. That store-bought Clamato is essential to getting that tomato flavor, and our salty, peppery garnish hits you with a kick so hard, even the homies who sipped a little too much gin and juice at the club the night before are gon' be a-OK.

✦

MAKES 6 TO 8 DRINKS

32 oz [960 ml] Clamato

8 oz [240 ml] vodka

4 tsp creamed horseradish

1 tsp Worcestershire sauce

1 tsp hot sauce, preferably Crystal

Salt and cracked black pepper

Celery stalks

Diced pepper Jack cheese

Kosher pickle spears

Pepperoncini

Pickled pearl onions

Stuffed olives

2 lemons, quartered

1. In a large pitcher, add the Clamato, vodka, horseradish, Worcestershire sauce, and hot sauce. Season with salt and pepper. Stir vigorously to combine.

2. Arrange the toppings in separate tumblers or old-fashioned glasses, with smaller items (such as olives, pepperoncini, pearl onions, and cheese) pre-skewered.

3. Pour the drinks into the glasses filled with ice. Squeeze a lemon quarter over each drink and drop it into the glass. Serve immediately.

MORNING-AFTER BLOODY BAR

Roll It Up 'Rito

SNOOP

A good blunt ain't the only thing the D.O. Double G knows how to roll up. We love our breakfast burritos out here on the West Coast. Can you blame us? It's basically breakfast rolled up in a hot, fluffy tortilla. Sounds like a winner to me! I love just about any breakfast burrito—from egg and cheese to potato and bacon—but the one I make at the crib has a special ingredient: Mexican chorizo. I know the Spanish stuff is delicious, but Mexican chorizo gives you that fresh texture you want. Oh, and don't forget: When it comes to hot sauce, we keep it Crystal up in here!

SERVES 2

4 eggs

2 Tbsp whole milk

¼ tsp salt

1 Tbsp plus 2 tsp vegetable oil

1 small russet potato (4 oz [115 g]), peeled and diced into ½ in [13 mm] cubes

½ cup [70 g] diced red onion

½ red bell pepper, diced

6 oz [170 g] fresh Mexican chorizo, casings removed

Two 10 in [25 cm] flour tortillas

½ cup [40 g] shredded Mexican four-cheese blend

½ cup [85 g] refried beans, warmed

¼ cup [65 g] salsa rojo

2 Tbsp chopped fresh cilantro

Hot sauce, preferably Crystal, for serving

CONTINUED ➜

1. In a small bowl, whisk together the eggs, milk, and salt until well combined. Set aside.

2. In a large nonstick skillet over medium-high heat, warm 1 Tbsp of the oil, then add the potato, onion, bell pepper, and 2 Tbsp of water. Cover and cook for 4 minutes. Uncover and continue to cook, stirring occasionally, until the onions and peppers are tender and the potatoes are golden brown and crisp, about 3 minutes more. Transfer to a bowl and set aside.

3. Return the skillet to medium-high heat and add the chorizo. Cook until crisp and browned, about 5 minutes, using a spatula to break up the meat into small chunks. Add the cooked chorizo to the potato mixture and wipe the pan clean with paper towels.

4. Return the skillet to medium-high heat and griddle the tortillas, one at a time, until soft and pliable, about 15 seconds per side. Transfer to a cutting board.

5. Lower the heat to medium and warm the remaining 2 tsp of oil in the skillet. Pour in the eggs and cook, using a heatproof spatula to slowly drag the edges of the egg toward the center of the pan, making large waves in the pan until the curds start to clump, 30 to 60 seconds. Lower the heat to low and add the cheese. Continue to cook until the curds are moist and almost set, about 30 seconds more.

6. Spread half of the refried beans down the center of each tortilla. Top each with half of the salsa, half of the potato-chorizo mixture, half of the scrambled eggs, and half of the cilantro. Fold the sides and ends of the tortilla over the filling and roll up tightly. Serve immediately, with the hot sauce.

Wake-and-Bake Meat Omelet

SNOOP

◆ Cali culture has given the world a lot. West Coast rap, Hollywood, and—yeah, we're damn proud of it—wake-and-bake living. It's part of the culture, and I love few things more than starting the day in a relaxed state of mind, enjoying that green the earth gave us.

◆ But here's the thing: A good wake and bake means you're going to be hungry. This hearty omelet has not one but two breakfast meats. I flavor my bacon and sausage with shallots, salt, and pepper and sprinkle the mixture with a bit of mozzarella. Place the hefty filling in the center of the omelet, and fold it in half with a spatula. You've got yourself a proper wake-and-bake omelet, goons.

SERVES 2

4 eggs

2 Tbsp whole milk

¼ tsp salt

¼ tsp cracked black pepper

3 slices bacon (not thick cut), cut crosswise into ¼ in [6 mm] pieces

2 breakfast sausage links, casings removed

1 shallot, thinly sliced

1 Tbsp vegetable oil

½ cup [40 g] shredded mozzarella cheese

1. In a small bowl, whisk together the eggs, milk, salt, and pepper until well combined and frothy. Set aside.

2. In a medium nonstick skillet over medium heat, fry the bacon until crispy, 7 to 8 minutes. Using a slotted spoon, transfer the bacon to a paper towel–lined plate.

3. Discard all but 2 tsp of the fat from the skillet and add the sausage and shallot. Cook until the sausage is no longer pink and the shallot is soft, using a spatula to break up the meat into crumbles, 5 to 6 minutes. Using a slotted spoon, transfer the sausage and shallot to the plate with the bacon. Wipe the pan clean with paper towels.

4. Add the oil to the skillet and return to medium heat, swirling the skillet to coat the bottom. Pour the egg mixture into the center and tilt the skillet in all directions to cover the bottom.

CONTINUED ➜

5. As the eggs start to set, using a heatproof spatula, gently lift the edges of the omelet toward the middle, letting the uncooked egg flow beneath the omelet and toward the edges of the skillet. The eggs are done when the bottom is set and the edges look crisp (the top will still look wet), 2 to 3 minutes.

6. Pour the meat mixture down the middle of the omelet and sprinkle the cheese on top. Cook for 30 seconds more.

7. With your spatula, fold the omelet in half. Tilt the skillet to slide the omelet toward the edge, then carefully transfer it to a plate. Serve immediately.

Fried Chicken and French Toast Sandwiches

E-40 + SNOOP

◆ We don't know what it is about chicken and bread, but the combination hits like none other. Tell us your mouth doesn't water just a little at the thought of chicken and biscuits from Popeyes, or chicken and waffles from Roscoe's, or a hot chicken sandwich from Nashville, Tennessee. We're a sucker for the combo and for decadence. It's how we came up with the next great chicken and bread combo: fried chicken and French toast.

◆ Like us, this sandwich is extravagant. You got your lavishly seasoned and deep-fried chicken breast, French toast gets bossed up with nutmeg and powdered sugar, and once the sandwich is put together? It's syrup overload, y'all. This isn't just decadent—it's also hella fun to make.

SERVES 4

FOR THE FRIED CHICKEN

½ cup [70 g] all-purpose flour

½ tsp salt

¼ tsp cracked black pepper

2 eggs

1 cup [80 g] finely crushed cornflakes

1 tsp garlic powder

Pinch of cayenne pepper

4 boneless, skinless chicken breasts, pounded ½ in [13 mm] thin

2 cups [480 ml] vegetable oil

FOR THE FRENCH TOAST

2 eggs

2 Tbsp whole milk

1 tsp vanilla extract

½ tsp ground nutmeg

3 Tbsp salted butter

8 slices sourdough bread

Confectioners' sugar, for serving

Maple syrup, for serving

TO MAKE THE FRIED CHICKEN

1. Set a wire rack over a baking sheet. In a shallow bowl, combine the flour, salt, and pepper. In a second bowl, beat the eggs with 1 Tbsp of water. In a third bowl, combine the cornflakes, garlic powder, and cayenne.

2. Dip a chicken breast first in the flour mixture, then in the eggs, and then in the cornflake mixture. Place the coated chicken on the wire rack and repeat with the remaining chicken breasts.

3. In a large cast-iron skillet over high heat, warm the oil until a deep-fry thermometer registers 375°F [190°C]. Carefully place the chicken breasts in the oil and cook for 5 minutes. Flip the chicken over and cook for 5 minutes more, until golden brown on both sides. Remove the chicken from the skillet and set aside.

TO MAKE THE FRENCH TOAST AND ASSEMBLE

1. In a shallow bowl, lightly whisk together the eggs, milk, vanilla, and nutmeg.

2. In a separate skillet over medium heat, melt the butter. Dip a slice of bread in the egg mixture, making sure to cover both sides, then place it in the skillet. Cook the first side, pressing down with a spatula, for 3 minutes or until deep golden brown. Flip the bread and cook the other side for 3 minutes, pressing down firmly, until golden brown. Repeat with the remaining bread slices.

3. Place each fried chicken breast between 2 slices of the French toast. Serve with confectioners' sugar and maple syrup.

FRIED CHICKEN AND FRENCH TOAST

SANDWICHES

Corned Beef
with All the Hash

E-40

That's right, we keep it heavy on the hash up in here! This is technically a breakfast dish, but corned beef with hash is so good, I sometimes throw this in the oven at night too. Corned beef is the centerpiece here, but the hash browns—shredded potatoes browned in the oven—are the foundation. Be careful when transferring the eggs into the wells—you want the yolk to keep its shape and the eggs to cook evenly. And y'all, I gotta ask, please be careful when taking the dish out of the oven and serving. Like that Cali sun all year round, it's going to be hot!

SERVES 4

5½ cups [470 g] shredded russet potatoes (or frozen, thawed, and patted dry)

2 cups [220 g] cooked and chopped shredded corned beef

½ cup [70 g] chopped yellow onion

½ cup [113 g] unsalted butter, melted

Salt and cracked black pepper

4 eggs

¼ cup [20 g] shredded Monterey Jack cheese

Heaping 1 Tbsp sliced green onions

Ketchup, for serving

Toast points, for serving

CONTINUED ➜

1. Preheat the oven to 400°F [200°C]. Lightly butter a 9 by 13 in [23 by 33 cm] baking dish or an 11 in [28 cm] skillet and set aside.

2. In a large mixing bowl, combine the potatoes, corned beef, onion, butter, and a pinch of salt and black pepper.

3. Transfer the mixture to the prepared baking dish and spread it out evenly. Make four evenly spaced wells using the bottom of a measuring cup or drinking glass.

4. Bake in the oven until the hash is golden brown on the sides and top, 45 to 50 minutes.

5. While the hash is baking, crack the eggs into separate small bowls. Remove the hash from the oven and carefully transfer each egg into one of the wells. Season with additional salt and pepper if desired. Sprinkle the hash evenly with the cheese.

6. Return the baking dish to the oven and bake until the whites of the egg are set, 8 to 10 minutes. Remove from the oven, sprinkle with the green onions, and serve immediately (the dish will be very hot—be careful!) with ketchup and toast points for dipping into the yolks.

Mochi Muffins with Pineapple and Coconut

E-40

◆ Mochi is one of those treats that we love. That gooey glutinous rice gives baked goods a texture that you just can't resist. These muffins are just as fun to look at as they are to eat, and I love getting to take Japanese mochi and give it that E-40 twist. Make a batch of these to go with your morning coffee, or better yet, make them part of one of my favorite Cali pastimes: wake and bake.

MAKES 12 MUFFINS

2 eggs

1 cup [240 ml] whole milk

1 tsp vanilla extract

2½ cups [350 g] mochiko rice flour

½ cup [100 g] granulated sugar

½ cup [100 g] packed light brown sugar

1 Tbsp matcha powder

1½ tsp baking powder

¼ tsp salt

¼ cup [55 g] unsalted butter, melted

¾ cup [180 ml] unsweetened coconut milk

½ cup [130 g] almond butter

½ cup [40 g] unsweetened coconut flakes

½ cup [85 g] chopped candied pineapple

CONTINUED ➜

1. Preheat the oven to 350°F [180°C]. Grease the wells of a twelve-cup muffin tin.

2. In a large bowl, whisk together the eggs, milk, and vanilla. In another large bowl, whisk together the rice flour, granulated sugar, brown sugar, matcha powder, baking powder, and salt.

3. Pour the wet ingredients into the dry ingredients and, using a wooden spoon, stir until well combined. Add the melted butter, coconut milk, and almond butter and mix until fully incorporated.

4. Pour the mixture into the prepared muffin pan, filling to just below the rim of each well. Sprinkle the coconut flakes and chopped candied pineapple evenly across the wells.

5. Bake until the muffins are set and golden brown on top, 20 to 25 minutes. Set the pan on a wire rack and let cool for 10 minutes before popping each muffin out to cool completely on the wire rack. Store in an airtight container at room temperature for up to 3 days.

'Naner Bread

SNOOP

✦ Don't throw those old bananas away, scrubs. Ripe bananas are just right for making this sweet, gently spiced 'naner bread, which is so fluffy, so chewy, and so comforting. I like my bread sweet, so along with a few ripe bananas, I add generous amounts of sugar, dark brown sugar, and honey to kick off my day. A cinnamon sugar topping will take you back to the easy days of eating a bowl of cereal before school. (The Dogg may have skipped class a few times, but you can bet I didn't ever skip breakfast!) Oh, and I know everybody has their preferences, but I like my banana bread nut-free! Chocolate chips on the other hand? Fill it up, son.

✦

SERVES 6 TO 8

FOR THE BREAD

1½ cups [210 g] all-purpose flour

½ cup [100 g] granulated sugar

½ cup [100 g] packed dark brown sugar

1 tsp ground cinnamon

1 tsp baking soda

½ tsp salt

2 or 3 very ripe bananas

½ cup [113 g] unsalted butter, melted

2 eggs

¼ cup [85 g] honey or molasses

¼ cup [60 ml] milk

¾ cup [135 g] chocolate chips

FOR THE TOPPING

¼ cup [50 g] packed dark brown sugar

2 Tbsp granulated sugar

2 tsp ground cinnamon

¼ tsp salt

TO MAKE THE BREAD

1. Preheat the oven to 350°F [180°C]. Butter and flour a 9 by 5 in [23 by 13 cm] loaf pan or line it with parchment paper, leaving at least a 2 in [5 cm] overhang on all sides.

2. In a medium bowl, combine the flour, granulated sugar, brown sugar, cinnamon, baking soda, and salt. In a large bowl, mash the bananas to a smooth paste with a fork. Whisk in the butter, eggs, honey, and milk until smooth. Add the flour mixture and stir until just combined. Stir in the chocolate chips. Pour the batter into the prepared pan.

TO MAKE THE TOPPING AND BAKE

1. In a small bowl, mix together the brown sugar, granulated sugar, cinnamon, and salt, using your fingers to break up any lumps. Sprinkle the mixture evenly over the batter.

2. Bake until a tester inserted into the center of the bread comes out clean, about 1 hour. Transfer to a wire rack to cool for at least 30 minutes before removing the bread from the pan. Cool completely on the rack before slicing. Wrap tightly and store at room temperature for up to 3 days.

'NANER BREAD

CHAPTER 2

MUNCHIES

Cajun-Spiced Potato Chips [43]

French Onion Just Dippin' [44]

Game Day Guac [47]

Fried Pickles [48]

Blazin' Jalapeño Poppers [52]

Turkey Sausage Scotch Eggs [55]

Air-Fryer Honey Walnut Shrimp [57]

Sticky Asian Chicken Wings [58]

Frito Pie [61]

Flamin' Hot Cheetos
Mac 'n' Cheese Bites [62]

Air-Fryer Pizza Alfredo [66]

Hot Link Air-Fryer Pizza [67]

Monte Cristo Sandwich [70]

Dungeness Crab Sandwich [72]

Man-ish Sandwich [73]

Cajun-Spiced Potato Chips

✦ There's plenty of good potato chips available at the grocery store, but it never hurts to add your own spice to those fried slices of heaven. I make this as easy as possible for you—no deep fryer necessary! Just pop the kettle chips in the oven while you make the seasoning, and after the chips have had a few minutes to heat up, hit them with the peppery herb mix.

✦

SERVES 6 TO 8

One 8½ oz [240 g] bag plain kettle-cooked potato chips

1 Tbsp paprika

1 tsp garlic powder

1 tsp onion powder

½ tsp sugar

¼ tsp dried thyme

¼ tsp dried basil

¼ tsp dried oregano

¼ tsp cracked black pepper

¼ tsp white pepper

¼ tsp cayenne pepper

1. Preheat the oven to 275°F [135°C]. Spread the chips in an even layer on a rimmed baking sheet, reserving the bag. Bake the chips until warm and slightly moist, about 7 minutes.

2. Meanwhile, in a small bowl, combine the paprika, garlic powder, onion powder, sugar, thyme, basil, oregano, black pepper, white pepper, and cayenne.

3. Remove the baking sheet from the oven and sprinkle the warm chips with the spice mixture. Carefully scoop the chips back into the bag and shake it gently to distribute the spices. Pour the seasoned chips into a large bowl and serve warm or at room temperature.

French Onion Just Dippin'

SNOOP

◆ I snack on Funyuns all the time, so it's crazy that it wasn't until I was an adult that I realized they add just the right crunch to a bowl of good French onion dip. You can use Flamin' Hot or regular Funyuns or even another type of chip—just make sure it's an onion snack so it complements the dip's flavors.

◆

SERVES 6 TO 8

1 Tbsp olive oil

1 Tbsp unsalted butter

2 medium red onions, finely chopped

2 garlic cloves, minced

1 tsp sugar

1 tsp salt

1 cup [240 g] sour cream

¼ cup [60 g] mayonnaise

1 bunch chives, minced

1 tsp Worcestershire sauce

Cracked black pepper

Funyuns, Flamin' Hot Funyuns, or other onion snack, crushed, for garnish (optional)

Potato chips, preferably ridged, for serving

1. In a medium skillet over medium-low heat, warm the oil and butter. Add the onions, garlic, sugar, and salt. Cook, stirring often, until caramelized and brown, about 45 minutes. Remove from the heat and let the onions cool to room temperature.

2. Meanwhile, in a large bowl, combine the sour cream, mayonnaise, half of the chives, and the Worcestershire sauce. Stir in the caramelized onions and season with pepper.

3. Sprinkle the Funyuns, if using, and the remaining chives on top of the dip and serve immediately with potato chips. The dip can be stored in an airtight container in the refrigerator for up to 3 days.

Game Day Guac

E-40

When the San Francisco Giants are stepping up to the plate, you can bet I'm grabbing some of my game day guac while watching Brandon Crawford do what he has to do for my city. Of course, I have to add a little heat, but you can seed the jalapeño so it's not too spicy. Serve it on game day, or enjoy it at the crib with the homies over the weekend.

SERVES 4 TO 6

2 medium avocados (8 oz [230 g] each), halved and pitted

1 Tbsp fresh lime juice

½ tsp salt, plus more as needed

1 garlic clove, minced

¼ cup [35 g] diced red onion

1 jalapeño, stemmed, seeded, and finely diced

1 plum tomato, seeded and diced

¼ cup [10 g] chopped fresh cilantro

Bowl-shaped tortilla chips or Fritos Scoops!, for serving

1. Using a spoon, scoop the avocado flesh in large chunks into a bowl. Add the lime juice, salt, and garlic and stir until combined. Smash the avocados with a fork until mostly mashed but with some chunks remaining.

2. Add the onion, jalapeño, tomato, and cilantro and stir until combined. Season with additional salt to taste.

3. Serve immediately with tortilla chips, or cover with plastic wrap pressed directly against the surface of the guacamole and refrigerate for up to 1 day.

Fried Pickles

✦ Don't make this one more complicated than it needs to be, goons. Bread those pickles and dredge them in the buttermilk. After that, you already know what to do: Drop 'em like it's hot in the frying oil, until they're nice and crispy and golden brown. And don't you even think about skipping that sauce. When you hit that sour cream and mayonnaise with the tomato flavor from the ketchup and heat from that Creole

✦ seasoning? You've got yourself a game day winner.

SERVES 4 TO 6

FOR THE SAUCE

¼ cup [60 g] mayonnaise

¼ cup [60 g] sour cream

1 Tbsp ketchup

¼ tsp Creole seasoning

FOR THE PICKLES

Vegetable oil, for frying

½ cup [70 g] all-purpose flour

½ cup [70 g] cornmeal

1 tsp onion powder

1 tsp Creole seasoning

¼ tsp cayenne pepper

¾ cup [180 ml] buttermilk

2 cups [350 g] hamburger dill pickle chips (or 12 dill pickle spears), drained and blotted dry with paper towels

TO MAKE THE SAUCE

In a small bowl, stir the mayonnaise, sour cream, ketchup, and Creole seasoning until combined. Set aside.

TO MAKE THE PICKLES

1. In a large Dutch oven over medium heat, warm about 1 in [2.5 cm] of vegetable oil to 350°F [180°C]. Line a baking sheet with paper towels and set aside.

2. While you heat the oil, in a large bowl, whisk together the flour, cornmeal, onion powder, Creole seasoning, and cayenne. Pour the buttermilk into a medium bowl.

3. Working a few pickle slices or spears at a time, dip the pickles in the flour mixture, shaking off the excess. Dredge the pickles in the buttermilk, allowing any excess to drip off. Return the pickles to the flour mixture until well coated, then transfer to a second, unlined baking sheet. Repeat until all of the pickles have been coated.

4. Carefully add half of the pickles to the hot oil and fry until golden brown and crispy, 1½ to 2 minutes, turning the slices halfway through frying. Adjust the heat to maintain a consistent 350°F [180°C] temperature.

5. Using a slotted spoon, transfer the pickles to the paper towel–lined baking sheet to drain. Repeat with the remaining pickles.

6. Serve immediately with the prepared sauce.

FRIED PICKLES

Blazin' Jalapeño Poppers

SNOOP

✦ There's more than one kind of blazin' I like to do, and it starts with some big, juicy jalapeños. When it comes to the munchies, I like to keep it simple, but I also want some heat. My jalapeño poppers are the solution. Instead of deep-frying these spicy bad boys, I bake them in the oven. Two cheeses—shredded Mexican four-cheese blend and cream cheese—bring maximum saltiness and creaminess, and generous strips
✦ of bacon swaddle these poppers in layers of salty pork flavor. Don't forget the chives, either. Never hurts to have a little extra green in your day, if you know what I mean . . .

SERVES 4 TO 6

12 medium jalapeños

1 Tbsp vegetable oil

½ cup [70 g] finely chopped yellow onion

½ tsp ground cumin

1 garlic clove, minced

1½ cups [120 g] shredded Mexican four-cheese blend

6 oz [170 g] cream cheese, at room temperature

2 Tbsp minced fresh cilantro

¼ cup [15 g] panko

12 slices bacon (not thick cut)

Chopped chives, for garnish (optional)

CONTINUED ➙

1. Preheat the oven to 450°F [230°C]. Line a baking sheet with aluminum foil and spray the foil with nonstick cooking spray.

2. Cut each pepper in half lengthwise. Scoop out the seeds and ribs using a small spoon; discard. Place the jalapeños cut-side up on the prepared baking sheet. Set aside.

3. In a medium nonstick skillet over medium heat, warm the oil. Add the onion and cook until softened and lightly browned, about 3 minutes. Add the cumin and garlic and cook until fragrant, about 1 minute. Transfer to a medium bowl.

4. Add the shredded cheese, cream cheese, and cilantro to the onion mixture, and stir until well combined.

5. Fill the jalapeño halves evenly with the cheese mixture, then sprinkle the tops with the panko. Cut each slice of bacon in half crosswise. Wrap each popper with a slice of bacon, using a toothpick to secure the bacon if necessary.

6. Bake until the peppers are tender, the cheese mixture is bubbling, and the bacon is crispy and brown, about 25 minutes. Let cool for 5 minutes, sprinkle the chopped chives on top, if desired, and serve.

Turkey Sausage Scotch Eggs

E-40

✦ I get it. I may not strike you as a dude who likes Scotch eggs. Well, guess what? Life is full of surprises, playas! I wrap my boiled egg in ground turkey instead of sausage, which makes it slightly healthier with a lighter yet still meaty texture. I hear that in Britain, where these little babies come from, they serve them with ranch dressing and hot mustard sauce. I'm a barbecue sauce man myself, but hey, whatever floats your boat.

MAKES 4

5 eggs

½ cup [70 g] all-purpose flour

Salt and cracked black pepper

1 cup [60 g] panko

6 oz [170 g] turkey breakfast sausage

Vegetable oil, for frying

Ketchup or mustard, for serving

1. Bring a medium pot three-quarters full of water to a boil over high heat. Carefully lower four of the eggs into the water. Lower the heat to medium and simmer the eggs for 7 minutes. Drain and place the eggs in a bowl. Cover with ice and let sit for 10 minutes. Peel the eggs and refrigerate until cold, at least 1 hour or up to 1 day.

2. Line a large plate with paper towels.

3. Whisk the remaining egg in a small bowl. Pour the flour into a separate bowl and season generously with salt and pepper. Place the panko into a third bowl.

4. Remove the sausages from their casings and divide the meat into four portions. Pat each quarter into a 6 in [15 cm] disc.

5. Wrap one egg in a disc of sausage, covering the egg in an even layer of meat. Dip into the whisked egg, roll in the flour, then roll in the panko, coating it completely. Set aside and repeat with the remaining eggs.

6. In a large skillet over medium-high heat, pour in oil to a depth of 2 in [5 cm]. Once the oil is shimmering, add the eggs, turning as needed, and cook until deep golden brown on all sides. Transfer to the paper towel–lined plate.

7. Serve hot or at room temperature, with ketchup or mustard for dipping.

Air-Fryer Honey Walnut Shrimp

E-40

◆ I find that one of the easiest ways to properly sweeten shrimp is to use honey. I picked this up from honey and walnut combos I've observed in many of my favorite Asian restaurants in San Francisco, Los Angeles, and the rest of California and figured out how to make at home. Don't forget that tangy dipping sauce.

◆

SERVES 4

¼ cup [60 g] mayonnaise

1 Tbsp sweetened condensed milk

1 Tbsp honey

1 Tbsp fresh lemon juice

1 cup [200 g] packed light brown sugar

1 cup [120 g] walnut halves

1 lb [455 g] large shrimp, peeled and deveined

½ tsp onion powder

½ tsp garlic powder

½ tsp salt

½ tsp cracked black pepper

¼ cup [35 g] cornstarch

Chopped green onions and lemon wedges, for garnish

1. Preheat the air fryer to 400°F [200°C]. Line a baking sheet with parchment paper.

2. In a medium bowl, combine the mayonnaise, condensed milk, honey, and lemon juice. Stir to combine, and set aside.

3. In a medium saucepan over medium-high heat, combine the brown sugar, 1 cup [240 ml] of water, and the walnuts. Bring the mixture to a boil and, maintaining a boil but reducing the heat if it starts to smoke or scorch, thicken it to a syrup. Spoon the walnut mixture onto the prepared baking sheet. Cool until firm and dry.

4. In a large bowl, sprinkle the shrimp with the onion powder, garlic powder, salt, and pepper. Add the cornstarch and toss to coat.

5. Carefully add the shrimp to the basket of the air fryer. Cook until golden brown, 3 to 5 minutes per side, turning halfway through cooking.

6. Toss the shrimp with the walnut mixture and serve immediately, garnished with green onions and lemon wedges, with the mayonnaise-lemon dipping sauce on the side.

Sticky Asian Chicken Wings

E-40

Despite what's sometimes communicated on television, Black Americans and Asian Americans have a lot of similarities, and our cultures intersect all the time on the West Coast. Here, my love of wings is complemented by my love of the Asian flavors I've been exposed to in California and beyond. My favorite thing about these wings is the sweet and spicy element. When you take a bite, you get a hit of saltiness from the soy sauce and sugary goodness from the brown sugar and honey. But give it just a second, playa. Because just when you think you've tasted it all, the wave of spicy sriracha hits you in the best possible way.

SERVES 4

FOR THE CHICKEN WINGS

3 lb [1.4 kg] chicken party wings (split into drumettes and wingettes, wingtips removed)

1 Tbsp vegetable oil

FOR THE SAUCE

2 Tbsp sesame seeds

¼ cup [60 ml] soy sauce

¼ cup [85 g] honey

2 Tbsp brown sugar

1 Tbsp sriracha

1 tsp toasted sesame oil

1 tsp rice vinegar

2 garlic cloves, minced

¼ tsp grated fresh ginger

1 green onion, thinly sliced, for garnish

CONTINUED ➡

TO MAKE THE CHICKEN WINGS

1. Preheat the oven to 450°F [230°C]. Line a baking sheet with aluminum foil and spray with nonstick cooking spray or brush lightly with the vegetable oil.

2. Pat the chicken wings dry with paper towels and arrange them evenly on the prepared baking sheet. Drizzle with the oil and toss to coat. Bake until golden brown and crisp, about 45 minutes, turning the wings over after 30 minutes.

TO MAKE THE SAUCE

1. In a small saucepan over medium heat, toast the sesame seeds until fragrant, about 4 minutes, stirring occasionally.

2. Add the soy sauce, honey, brown sugar, sriracha, sesame oil, vinegar, garlic, and ginger to the pan. Increase the heat to high and bring to a boil, then lower the heat to medium and simmer until the sauce is syrupy and coats the back of a spoon, 3 to 4 minutes, stirring occasionally.

TO FINISH THE WINGS

Place the wings in a large bowl, pour the sauce on top, and, with tongs, toss until evenly coated. Transfer the wings to a serving platter and sprinkle with the green onion. Serve immediately.

Frito Pie

E-40

It seems like everybody has a Frito pie story from childhood. Even though the Frito pie comes from Texas (though some New Mexicans disagree), it's in food courts, school cafeterias, and sports arenas across the country. The Frito pie is messy, over the top, and full of a lot of stuff the doc might not be a fan of, but as far as I'm concerned, ain't no better way to be.

SERVES 4

Four 1¼ oz [35 g] bags Fritos Chili Cheese corn chips

One 14 oz [400 g] can beef chili with beans

2 cups [160 g] shredded Mexican-style four-cheese blend

¼ cup [60 g] sour cream

Hot sauce, cilantro leaves, shredded lettuce, and chopped tomato, optional, for topping

1. Using scissors, snip one corner off the top of one bag of Fritos. Press down on the bag to lightly crumble the chips inside. With the scissors, cut so the bag forms an open pocket. Repeat with the remaining bags.

2. Add ¼ cup [60 g] of the chili, ¼ cup [20 g] of the cheese, 1 tablespoon of the sour cream, and any preferred toppings to one bag. Repeat with the remaining bags.

3. Using a spoon, stir to combine the mixture inside each bag, then enjoy immediately.

Flamin' Hot Cheetos Mac 'n' Cheese Bites

SNOOP

✦ Let me introduce you to another game day delight: Flamin' Hot Cheetos Mac 'n' Cheese Bites. You heard that right, goons. I figured out how to take everybody's favorite dish from their grandma, mom, and auntie and combined it with every former public school kid's favorite after-school snack. These fried bites are as spicy and gooey as you can imagine, so I suggest serving them with a ranch or blue cheese dip to cool 'em down. Or get creative. Ketchup, BBQ sauce, or hell, forget what I say and

✦ make 'em even hotter by serving them with hot sauce—there's no limit!

SERVES 6 TO 8

Salt

1 lb [455 g] elbow macaroni

2 cups [480 ml] whole milk

1 cup [240 ml] heavy cream

4 Tbsp [55 g] unsalted butter, plus more for greasing

1¼ cups [175 g] all-purpose flour

2½ cups [200 g] shredded extra-sharp Cheddar cheese

2 tsp Worcestershire sauce

2 tsp dry mustard

1 tsp cracked black pepper

½ tsp ground nutmeg

¼ tsp cayenne pepper

Vegetable oil, for frying

2 cups [110 g] Flamin' Hot Cheetos

4 eggs, lightly beaten

Ranch dressing or blue cheese dip, for serving

CONTINUED ➙

1. Lightly butter a 9 by 13 in [23 by 33 cm] baking dish and set aside.

2. Bring a large pot of heavily salted water to a boil. Add the macaroni and cook until al dente, about 1 minute less than the time in the package instructions. Drain and set aside.

3. In a small saucepan over medium heat, warm the milk and cream, being careful not to boil it.

4. Meanwhile, in a large skillet over medium heat, melt the butter. Sprinkle in ¼ cup [35 g] of the flour and whisk constantly for 2 to 3 minutes. Gradually whisk in the warmed milk mixture. Cook, whisking frequently, for 2 minutes, or until thickened and smooth. (Adjust the heat to keep the milk from boiling.)

5. Gradually add the cheese, whisking until fully incorporated and smooth. Add the Worcestershire sauce, mustard, black pepper, nutmeg, and cayenne. Season with salt.

6. Add the cooked macaroni to the cheese sauce and stir until combined. Spoon the mixture into the prepared baking dish. Let it cool to room temperature and then transfer to the refrigerator until firm, 3 to 4 hours or overnight.

7. When ready to fry the balls, line a baking sheet with paper towels. In a large saucepan over high heat, warm about ½ in [13 mm] of vegetable oil.

8. Place the Cheetos in a large ziplock plastic bag and, using a rolling pin, crush into a crumbly consistency.

9. Arrange three shallow bowls and place the remaining 1 cup [140 g] of flour, the eggs, and crushed Cheetos into separate bowls.

10. Using an ice cream scoop, scoop 1½ to 2 in [4 to 5 cm] wide balls from the baking dish of mac and cheese onto a plate.

11. Chill the balls in the freezer for 5 minutes.

12. Roll one ball in the flour, shaking off any excess, then dip it in the egg, covering all sides. Lastly, roll it in the crumbled Cheetos. Shake off any excess and repeat with the rest of the balls.

13. In batches, fry the balls, turning to fry all sides, until just crispy and golden, 2 to 3 minutes. Transfer the fried mac and cheese balls to the paper towel–lined baking sheet to drain. Serve immediately with ranch dressing or blue cheese dip.

Air-Fryer Pizzas

E-40

✦ The millennials may think they have the air fryer on lock, but this Bay Area native knows a thing or two about how to make this *Back to the Future*–lookin' contraption do some dope things too. I can't help but plug my Goon with the Spoon chicken and beef sausage links here, which add the traditional Italian meat taste that we all love about pizza. Once you've got your toppings set, skip the big ol' brick oven and pop it in the air fryer for a pie that's done so fast, you'll never need to order out again.

✦

Air-Fryer Pizza Alfredo

SERVES 2

4 slices bacon

One 10 oz [285 g] package (two 8 in [20 cm]) mini pizza crusts

½ cup [120 ml] store-bought Alfredo sauce

1 cup [80 g] shredded mozzarella cheese

¼ cup [55 g] halved cherry tomatoes

1 small red onion, sliced into rings

Italian seasoning, grated Parmesan cheese, red pepper flakes, and chopped basil leaves, for serving (optional)

1. In a skillet, cook the bacon until crisp, 3 to 4 minutes. Break into pieces.

2. Preheat the air fryer to 375°F [190°C]. Place one pizza crust in the fryer, bottom-side up. Cook until lightly browned, about 3 minutes. Flip over and continue to cook 3 minutes more.

3. Spread half of the Alfredo sauce over the pizza crust. Top with half of the cheese, bacon, tomatoes, and onion. Return to the air fryer and bake until the cheese is melted and the crust is crisp, 2 to 3 minutes more.

4. Transfer the pizza to a clean surface. Repeat with the remaining Alfredo sauce, bacon, cheese, tomatoes, and onion to assemble and cook the second pizza. Sprinkle with Italian seasoning, grated Parmesan, red pepper flakes, and basil, if desired. Cut into slices and serve immediately.

Hot Link Air-Fryer Pizza

SERVES 2

One 10 oz [285 g] package
(two 8 in [20 cm]) mini
pizza crusts

½ cup [120 ml] pizza sauce

12 oz [340 g] precooked
hot beef sausage links,
preferably Goon with the
Spoon brand, cut into ¼ in
[6 mm] slices

2 cups [160 g] shredded
mozzarella cheese

1 green, orange, or yellow
bell pepper, chopped

¼ cup [35 g] sliced black
olives

Grated Parmesan cheese
and red pepper flakes, for
serving (optional)

1. Preheat the air fryer to 375°F
   [190°C]. Place one pizza
   crust in the fryer, bottom-
   side up. Cook until lightly
   browned, about 3 minutes.
   Flip over and continue to
   cook 3 minutes more.

2. Spread half of the pizza
   sauce over the pizza crust.
   Top with half of the sausage,
   cheese, bell pepper, and
   olives. Return to the air fryer
   and bake until the cheese is
   melted and the crust is crisp,
   2 to 3 minutes more.

3. Transfer the pizza to a clean
   surface. Repeat with the
   remaining sauce, sausage,
   cheese, bell pepper, and
   olives to assemble and cook
   the second pizza. Sprinkle
   with grated Parmesan and
   red pepper flakes, if desired.
   Cut into slices and serve
   immediately.

AIR-FRYER PIZZAS

Monte Cristo Sandwich

E-40

Now look. I've been lucky enough to travel around, and I've had some boss sandwiches around the world. Philly cheesesteaks in Philly, po'boys and muffulettas in New Orleans, even panini in Italy! Nothing—and I mean nothing!—compares to a Monte Cristo sandwich. French toast may be from Paris, but once Americans got their hands on it? Whooo wee! We took it and made it our own, and that's exactly what I do here. Those hot, melted layers of ham and cheese bring an OG like me nothing but joy. Don't forget to serve the sandwich with some strawberry or raspberry jam for a truly sweet and savory bite.

MAKES 1 SANDWICH

2 tsp Dijon mustard

3 slices white sandwich bread

1 to 3 Tbsp salted butter, at room temperature

2 thin slices deli ham

2 thin slices deli turkey

2 slices Swiss cheese

1 egg

¼ cup [60 ml] whole milk

Confectioners' sugar, for dusting

Strawberry or raspberry jam, for serving

1. Divide the mustard between two slices of bread, spreading it to the edges. Butter the remaining slice of bread on both sides with 1 Tbsp of the butter. Place one slice of bread on your work surface, mustard-side up. Layer with one slice of ham, one slice of turkey, and one slice of cheese. Top with the buttered slice of bread, then the remaining ham, turkey, and cheese. Top with the remaining slice of bread, mustard-side down.

2. In a medium bowl, whisk together the egg and milk.

3. If using a skillet, set over medium heat and add the remaining 2 Tbsp butter. If using an air fryer, preheat it.

4. Dip the sandwich in the milk mixture, allowing each side to soak for 15 to 30 seconds.

5. If using a skillet, place the sandwich in the skillet and cook 3 to 4 minutes per side, until golden brown on both sides.

6. If using an air fryer, set the timer on the air fryer to 8 minutes and place the sandwich in the cooking basket. Cook until golden brown on both sides, flipping after 4 minutes.

7. Dust the warm sandwich with confectioners' sugar, slice it in half diagonally, and serve with jam on the side.

Dungeness Crab Sandwich

E-40

✦ This ain't no play-around cookin' right here. Dungeness crab meat isn't cheap, so this is the type of sandwich you want to make when you're really treatin' yourself or your loved ones. Crab is great on its own, but the real star of the sandwich is the herb butter, which infuses chives and parsley into the Texas toast, giving you really fresh
✦ coastal flavors.

MAKES 2 SANDWICHES

FOR THE HERB BUTTER

1 Tbsp minced fresh chives and parsley

4 Tbsp [55 g] salted butter, at room temperature

FOR THE SANDWICH

1 cup [150 g] jumbo lump crabmeat, preferably Dungeness

3 Tbsp fresh lemon juice

2 Tbsp mayonnaise, preferably Best Foods

½ tsp salt

4 slices Texas toast or other thickly sliced white bread

Lemon wedges, for serving

TO MAKE THE HERB BUTTER

In a small bowl, with a fork, mash the herbs into the butter until well combined.

TO MAKE THE SANDWICH

1. In a large mixing bowl, combine the crabmeat, lemon juice, mayonnaise, and salt. Fold gently to combine.

2. Spread the bread slices on both sides with herb butter, dividing it evenly among the slices. In a large nonstick skillet over medium-high heat, toast the bread until golden brown, 2 to 3 minutes per side. Remove the bread to a platter.

3. Top two slices of bread with the crab mixture, dividing it evenly between the slices and spreading it to the edges. Top with the second two slices of bread, slice the sandwiches on the diagonal, and serve hot, with the lemon wedges on the side.

Man-ish Sandwich

E-40

✦ My man-ish sandwich may look like a hamburger, but what differentiates it from the American classic is a gift from down south: Texas toast. Swap those hamburger buns with thick garlic- and butter-infused pieces of toast and you've got yourself a sandwich fit for a king.

MAKES 2 SANDWICHES

½ lb [230 g] ground beef

Salt and cracked black pepper

Vegetable oil, for cooking

2 slices Swiss cheese

4 slices Texas toast or other thickly sliced white bread

1 Tbsp mayonnaise, preferably Best Foods

1 tsp yellow mustard

1. Place the ground beef in a large bowl. Season generously with salt and pepper, then form two round patties of equal size.

2. Place a large cast-iron skillet or stovetop grill pan over medium-high heat. When hot, brush the cooking surface with vegetable oil. Add the patties and sear until brown or grill marks form, about 4 minutes. Flip, and then top with the cheese slices. Cook an additional 3 or 4 minutes, until the other side is brown.

3. Meanwhile, place a large nonstick skillet over medium-high heat. Brush the cooking surface with oil, then add the bread and cook until toasted on one side, 2 to 3 minutes. Turn off the heat, spread two slices of the bread with the mayo and mustard, and place the patties on top. Top with the additional slice of bread, toasted-side up. Press down on the sandwich with a spatula. Slice the sandwiches on the diagonal and serve warm.

CHAPTER 3

DRINKS

E-40 Water [77]

Pool Party Punch [78]

Cali Sangria [80]

Scorpion Bowl [81]

Spritzers: 19 Crimes
& Earl Stevens Special [84]

Pimp's Cup [87]

Calvin's Grape Juice [88]

Grape Juice Cocktail [89]

Beach City Iced Tea [92]

Tini with a Twist [95]

E-40 Water

✦ There's water, then there's E-40 Water. As you may have guessed, this ain't H_2O. Unlike my sports drink I used to sell on the West Coast, this drink is boozy, fruity, and full of flavor. This drink is as fresh as they come, from the lemon, lime, and mango juices to the mango spears used for garnish. Refresh ya'selves the E-40 way—you won't be disappointed.

SERVES 2

4 oz [120 ml] vodka

4 oz [120 ml] mango juice

1 oz [30 ml] fresh
lemon juice

1 oz [30 ml] fresh
lime juice

2 oz [60 ml] malt
liquor beverage

2 oz [60 ml] mango-
flavored soda

Ripe mango spears,
for garnish (optional)

Mint sprigs, for garnish
(optional)

1. Pour the vodka, mango juice, lemon juice, and lime juice into a cocktail shaker and shake well to combine. Fill two highball glasses with ice and pour the juice mixture into the glasses. Pour 1 oz [30 ml] of the malt liquor and mango soda into each glass and stir.

2. Garnish with mango spears and mint sprigs, if desired.

Pool Party Punch

E-40 + SNOOP

When the days are long and hot, we like to cool off and chill out with our pool party punch, the freshest way to stay refreshed on the West Coast. We personally like lemonade in our summertime punch, but whatever fresh juice floats your boat works here. Don't forget those orange, lemon, and strawberry slices for garnish. It's the summertime, y'all! Get festive!

MAKES 6 TO 8 DRINKS

16 oz [480 ml] cranberry cocktail

16 oz [480 ml] orange juice

4 oz [120 ml] lemonade

6 oz [180 ml] vodka

Orange slices, for garnish

Lemon slices, for garnish

Strawberry slices, for garnish

Club soda, for serving (optional)

1. In a large punch bowl filled with ice, mix together the cranberry cocktail, orange juice, lemonade, and vodka.

2. Garnish with orange, lemon, and strawberry slices. When serving, top off each drink with a splash of club soda, if desired.

Cali Sangria

E-40 + SNOOP

We came up with a pretty good take on sangria out here in Cali. Snoop's 19 Crimes Red is the wine foundation here, and lemons, berries, and oranges are always a good bet for any pitcher of sangria. But y'all know we like to keep it 'hood at home, so we hit our drink with Hennessy to add a deep, rich, earthy flavor to the fruity beverage. I know, I know, it's not Spanish, but neither are we goons! Don't knock it till you've tried it.

MAKES 6 TO 8 DRINKS

1 large orange, half sliced into rounds, half juiced

1 lemon, sliced into rounds

1 cup [120 to 160 g] sliced fruit, such as apple, strawberries or other berries, grapes, kiwi, or stone fruit

4 oz [120 ml] Hennessy

1 Tbsp honey

One bottle 19 Crimes Snoop Dogg Cali Red Blend or other bright, fruity red wine

Club soda, for serving (optional)

1. In a large pitcher, combine the orange slices, orange juice, lemon slices, sliced fruit, Hennessy, and honey. Pour in the wine and stir to combine.

2. Chill for up to 24 hours or serve immediately over ice. Top with club soda, if desired.

Scorpion Bowl

✦ Warning playas! This drink is heavy on the liquor; be careful! Back when we used to throw parties with some of our favorite rappers, Scorpion Bowls would also help get the party started. It's not a Scorpion Bowl without at least four different liquors, so unsurprisingly, this is a drink you want to sip on slowly.

✦

MAKES 6 TO 8 DRINKS

8 oz [240 ml] orange juice

6 oz [180 ml] pineapple juice

6 oz [180 ml] passion fruit juice

2 oz [60 ml] gin

2 oz [60 ml] dark rum

2 oz [60 ml] light rum

2 oz [60 ml] vodka

2 oz [60 ml] grenadine

Juice from 1 lemon

Orange slices, for garnish

Maraschino cherries, for garnish

1. In a scorpion bowl or large punch bowl filled with ice, mix together the orange juice, pineapple juice, passion fruit juice, gin, dark rum, light rum, vodka, grenadine, and lemon juice.

2. Garnish with orange slices and maraschino cherries. Serve immediately.

SCORPION BOWL

SPRITZERS:
19 Crimes

E-40 + SNOOP

✦ Chocolate or vanilla, cedar or oak, blackberries or cherries: These are all flavors in my 19 Crimes. Whatever you taste, you good, and the fizz makes it even better.

✦

MAKES 1 DRINK

3 oz [90 ml] 19 Crimes Snoop Dogg Cali Red Blend or other bright, fruity red wine, chilled

3 oz [90 ml] cold club soda or seltzer

1 thin orange slice or one 1 in [2.5 cm] strip orange peel

1. Pour the wine into a wine glass or flute. Gently pour the club soda on top.

2. Run the orange slice or peel around the rim of the glass, then float it in the drink. Serve immediately.

SPRITZERS:
Earl Stevens Special

◆ Best when ice cold, club soda softens the sweet, voluptuous mango . . .

◆

MAKES 1 DRINK

3 oz [90 ml] Earl Stevens
Mangoscato or other
bright white wine, chilled

3 oz [90 ml] cold club soda
or seltzer

1 thin orange slice
or one 1 in [2.5 cm] strip
orange peel

1. Pour the wine into a wine
   glass or flute. Gently pour
   the club soda on top.

2. Run the orange slice or peel
   around the rim of the glass,
   then float it in the drink.
   Serve immediately.

Pimp's Cup

SNOOP

People assume rappers only like things that are serious, heavy, and intense. Well, I got news for you: The D.O. Double G loves a light beverage every now and then. When I want something sweet and refreshing, I make this cocktail. Try serving it in glasses that are filled with half lemonade and half black tea for a boozy riff on an Arnold Palmer.

MAKES 1 DRINK

6 oz [180 ml] Pimm's

2 oz [60 ml] fresh lemon juice

1 tsp sugar

2 orange slices

1 strawberry, sliced

Mint sprig

Ginger ale, for topping off

1. Fill a cocktail shaker with ice. Add the Pimm's, lemon juice, and sugar. Cover the shaker and shake well for 30 seconds.

2. In a tumbler, drop in the orange slices, strawberry slices, mint sprig, and ice. Strain the Pimm's mixture into the prepared tumbler until halfway full and top off with ginger ale. Serve immediately.

Calvin's Grape Juice

SNOOP

Real ones know that Kool-Aid is one of the best drinks on the planet. This beverage is a more grown-up take on the drink. I pair my grape juice with a nice lemon-and-lime mixture to give it a kick, and any liquor works well with the mix. And don't get it twisted: The Dogg has mad love for all my alcohol-free homies—feel free to make this a mocktail or cocktail.

MAKES 6 TO 8 DRINKS

½ cup [100 g] Kool-Aid Grape Drink Mix powder

12 oz [360 ml] gin (optional)

2 oz [60 ml] fresh lemon juice

2 oz [60 ml] fresh lime juice

Sparkling lemon water, for topping off

1. In a large pitcher, mix the drink mix with 6 cups [1.4 L] of water until the powder dissolves. Add the gin (if using), lemon juice, and lime juice and stir to combine.

2. To serve, ladle into punch cups or tumblers filled with ice. Top off each cup with a splash of sparkling lemon water. Serve immediately.

Grape Juice Cocktail

✦ An elevated version of standard Kool-Aid, this drink gets its kick from fresh lime juice. It can easily be made boozy or alcohol-free, depending on your preference. Feel free to use your favorite alcohol in place of the vodka.

✦

MAKES 1 DRINK

2 oz [60 ml] Concord grape juice

1 oz [30 ml] vodka

½ oz [15 ml] Chambord

Juice from 1 lime

1. Fill a cocktail shaker with ice. Add the grape juice, vodka, Chambord, and lime juice. Cover the shaker and shake well for 30 seconds.

2. Strain into a rocks glass or mason jar filled with ice. Serve immediately.

GRAPE JUICE

COCKTAIL

Beach City Iced Tea

✦ We hit our Long Island Iced Tea with a Long Beach twist. Careful with this one. It'll get you twisted quick!

✦

MAKES 1 DRINK

2 oz [60 ml] cranberry juice

½ oz [15 ml] vodka

½ oz [15 ml] light rum

½ oz [15 ml] blanco tequila

½ oz [15 ml] gin

½ oz [15 ml] triple sec

Orange slice,
for garnish

Lemon slice,
for garnish

1. Fill a cocktail shaker with ice. Add the cranberry juice, vodka, rum, tequila, gin, and triple sec. Cover the shaker and shake well for 30 seconds.

2. Strain into a highball glass filled with ice and garnish with an orange slice and a lemon slice. Serve immediately.

Tini with a Twist

E-40

✦ This tini wini cocktail is twisted with vodka, pineapple juice, lime, and orchids, one of my favorite flowers. The ladies, fellas, and everyone will be able to find something to love about this bright favorite.

✦

MAKES 1 DRINK

3 oz [90 ml] vodka

1 oz [30 ml] pineapple juice

Juice from 1 lime

Lime twist, for garnish

Orchid, for garnish

1. Chill a martini glass.

2. Fill a cocktail shaker with ice. Add the vodka, pineapple juice, and lime juice. Cover the shaker and shake well for 30 seconds.

3. Strain into the chilled martini glass. Garnish with the lime twist and orchid and serve immediately.

MAINS

Gumbo

I only spent about a year living in Louisiana, but even in that short time I learned just how important gumbo is to the state's culture and foodways. There's no denying that the best gumbo on the planet is probably going to be at someone's home in Louisiana, but the restaurants have some serious game too. Just thinkin' about a bowl from Li'l Dizzy's Cafe, where they make their own homemade sausage, or that Creole gumbo at Dooky Chase's has me wanting to get back to the Big Easy right now!

I learned so much from the time I lived in and traveled to Louisiana, and from my mother, who grew up around all of the crab, shrimp, and other seafood you find in gumbo. To me, gumbo is a celebratory meal, something to enjoy with your day-ones—the folks you truly love and know got your back. If you're familiar with gumbo, you'll see a lot of classic elements in this recipe, like the Holy Trinity of Creole cooking—celery, bell peppers, and onion—and roux, a mixture of fat and flour that thickens soups and stews. It's a time-consuming dish, but the results are well worth the effort.

SERVES 4, WITH LEFTOVERS

1 cup [240 ml] vegetable oil

1 cup [140 g] all-purpose flour

1 cup [140 g] chopped onion

1 cup [120 g] chopped green or red bell pepper

1 cup [120 g] chopped celery

1 cup [150 g] diced tomatoes

12 oz [340 g] hot beef sausage links, preferably Goon with the Spoon brand, cut into 1 in [2.5 cm] pieces

2 Tbsp Cajun seasoning

1 tsp chopped garlic

1 tsp cracked black pepper

6 cups [1.4 L] chicken stock

1 lb [455 g] large shrimp, peeled and deveined

2 cups [295 g] cooked shredded chicken

1 cup [130 g] sliced okra

2 Tbsp filé powder (optional)

Chopped parsley, for garnish (optional)

1. In a Dutch oven over medium heat, combine the oil and flour. Cook, stirring constantly, until the mixture is thick and the color of peanut butter, about 30 minutes.

2. Stir in the onion, bell pepper, celery, and tomatoes. Cook and stir until softened, about 5 minutes. Add the sausage and cook, stirring occasionally, until browned, about 5 minutes. Add the Cajun seasoning, garlic, and pepper. Cook until fragrant, about 2 minutes.

3. Add the chicken stock, reduce the heat to low, and simmer for 30 minutes. Add the shrimp, chicken, and okra. Simmer until the shrimp is pink and cooked through, about 10 minutes. Stir in the filé powder, if using, and serve immediately, garnished with chopped parsley, if desired.

GUMBO

Crab Boil

Crab boils are as American as they come. Folks enjoy a good crab boil down south, and there's nothing like being in community with the ones you love around some damn good seafood. Everybody has their favorite seasonings and marinades for crab boils, like Tony Chachere's Original Creole Seasoning and Old Bay. Like a real gangsta, I keep my crab boils 100 with E. Cuarenta Cerveza lager. It might seem strange to use beer in a crab boil, but beer is pretty common when cooking with seafood because it adds a crispiness to the texture and makes fried seafood even crunchier. Here, the Mexican lager really brings out the flavor of the crab and makes for a perfect bite.

SERVES 6

3 Tbsp vegetable oil

12 oz [340 g] hot beef sausage links, preferably Goon with the Spoon brand, cut into 1 in [2.5 cm] pieces

20 cipollini onions, halved

8½ cups [2 L] Mexican lager, preferably E. Cuarenta Cerveza

1 lb [455 g] small red potatoes

¼ cup [60 ml] liquid crab boil seasoning

1 Tbsp salt

1 tsp hot sauce

1 tsp cracked black pepper

3 fresh bay leaves

1 jalapeño, sliced

2 ears yellow corn, cut into thirds

3 lb [1.4 kg] live crab, cleaned

Sliced green onions, lemon wedges, and red pepper flakes, for garnish (optional)

1. In a large stockpot, heat the oil over medium heat and sauté the sausage and onions until browned, about 5 minutes.

2. Add the 3 cups [720 ml] water, the beer, potatoes, crab boil seasoning, salt, hot sauce, pepper, bay leaves, and jalapeños. Cover the pot and bring to a boil.

3. Reduce the heat to medium-low, add the corn, and cover. Cook until the corn is tender, about 10 minutes. Add the crab and cook about 7 minutes. Using a colander, drain the contents of the pot.

4. Plate immediately on a large serving dish or spread newspapers on a table and scatter the ingredients on top. Garnish with green onions, lemon wedges, and red pepper flakes, if desired.

Ridin' Dirty Shrimp 'n' Grits

E-40 + SNOOP

Shrimp and grits are another dish we have to thank the South for. Our ancestors would use the shrimp they caught while working for their slave owners and cook them alongside their rations of grits. Eventually this dish became a Southern staple, and it's all over brunch menus down south, especially at some of our favorite Black-owned restaurants.

Just as Black folks have moved around the country, so too has our food. It's pretty easy to find shrimp and grits on menus at American restaurants in LA and the Bay Area, but it's something special to make them at home. We like to add a little crunch to our shrimp and grits, so make sure to fry that bacon hard!

SERVES 4

FOR THE GRITS

1 Tbsp unsalted butter

1 cup [140 g] stone-ground grits (not instant)

2 cups [480 ml] low-sodium chicken broth

1 cup [240 ml] whole milk

¼ tsp salt

1 cup [80 g] shredded sharp Cheddar cheese

FOR THE SHRIMP

4 slices bacon (not thick cut), cut crosswise into ½ in [13 mm] pieces

1 lb [455 g] 21/25-count shrimp, peeled and deveined

3 green onions, thinly sliced, with 1 Tbsp dark green parts reserved for garnish

2 tsp hot sauce, preferably Crystal

Salt and cracked black pepper

TO MAKE THE GRITS

1. In a medium saucepan over medium heat, melt the butter. Add the grits and cook until lightly toasted, about 2 minutes. Add the chicken broth, milk, and salt. Increase the heat to medium-high and bring to a boil.

2. Lower the heat to medium-low, cover, and simmer, stirring occasionally, until thick and creamy, 30 to 40 minutes. Remove the pot from the heat and stir in the cheese. Cover to keep warm.

TO COOK THE SHRIMP

1. In a large skillet over medium heat, add the bacon and cook until browned and crisp, 7 to 8 minutes, turning once halfway through cooking. Meanwhile, line a large plate with paper towels. Using a slotted spoon, transfer the bacon to the paper towel–lined plate. Discard all but 1 Tbsp of the fat from the skillet.

2. Increase the heat to medium-high and add the shrimp and the green onions. Cook until the shrimp is pink and opaque throughout, 4 to 5 minutes. Remove from the heat, stir in the bacon and hot sauce, and season with salt and pepper.

3. Ladle the grits into individual bowls and top with the shrimp. Garnish with the reserved green onions and serve.

Grits with Crispy Fish

E-40

Grits are extremely versatile. A staple of the kitchen, the boiled cornmeal is typically served at breakfast with eggs and bacon and, of course, shrimp. I love a good plate of shrimp and grits and realized that fish works really great with the dish as well. I batter my cod with panko so it's got a good firm crust to stand up to the porridge, and top it with crunchy fish and a lemony sauce.

SERVES 4

Grits from Ridin' Dirty Shrimp 'n' Grits (page 104)

Air-Fryer Panko Cod with Lemon (page 108)

Lemon wedges

1. Prepare the grits according to the method for Ridin' Dirty Shrimp 'n' Grits through step 2 (page 105).

2. Prepare the cod according to the method for the Air-Fryer Panko Cod with Lemon through step 3 (page 108).

3. To serve, ladle the grits into individual bowls and top with the cod. Drizzle with the lemon-butter sauce for the cod and serve with lemon wedges.

Air-Fryer Panko Cod with Lemon

SERVES 4

1 cup [60 g] panko

1 tsp chopped garlic

½ tsp salt

¼ tsp cracked black pepper

4 cod fillets (about 1 lb [455 g] total)

8 Tbsp [113 g] butter

3 Tbsp fresh lemon juice

1 Tbsp heavy cream

1 Tbsp chopped parsley

1 Tbsp finely grated lemon zest

Parsley leaves and lemon slices, for garnish (optional)

1. Preheat the air fryer to 400°F [200°C].

2. In a shallow bowl, combine the panko, garlic, salt, and pepper. Dip each piece of cod into the panko mixture, then lightly press down to adhere. Flip and coat the other side. Place directly in the basket of the air fryer and bake until the fish is opaque and flakes when tested with a fork, 10 to 15 minutes.

3. Meanwhile, in a medium skillet over medium-low heat, whisk together the butter, lemon juice, and cream until combined and slightly thickened, about 3 minutes. Stir in the parsley and lemon zest and remove from the heat.

4. To serve, transfer the fillets to individual plates and drizzle each with the lemon-butter sauce. Garnish with parsley sprigs and lemon wedges, if desired.

Chippin' and Dippin' Fried Chicken

SNOOP

✦ By now, y'all can tell that chips are my thing. If I can find a way to add a bag of Funyuns, Fritos, or Doritos to somethin', I'll do it. That's exactly what I've done with my favorite recipe for fried chicken. This isn't your typical flour-based breading, scrubs. Chicken is coated in a batter made from flour and Frito corn chips and fried until crispy and golden brown. While I like to get experimental with my batters, I'm a creature of habit when it comes to my dipping sauces. Crystal hot sauce only for me, folks!

✦

SERVES 4 TO 6

3½ lb [1.6 kg] whole chicken, cut into 10 pieces (2 wings, 2 drumsticks, 2 breasts cut crosswise, 2 thighs)

2 cups [480 ml] buttermilk

2 cups [280 g] all-purpose flour

1½ cups [150 g] crushed Fritos corn chips

2 tsp salt, plus more for seasoning

1 tsp cracked black pepper, plus more for seasoning

1 tsp cayenne pepper

Vegetable oil, for frying

Hot sauce, preferably Crystal, for serving (optional)

1. Season the chicken pieces generously with salt and black pepper. In a large bowl, soak the chicken in the buttermilk for at least 15 minutes or up to overnight in the refrigerator.

2. In a large bowl, stir together the flour, crushed corn chips, salt, black pepper, and cayenne until combined. Put the bowl with the buttermilk and chicken next to the flour mixture. Put a wire rack or pan next to the two bowls; this will be where you set your battered chicken.

3. Lift one piece of chicken out of the buttermilk and let any excess drip back into the bowl. Roll the chicken in the flour mixture, coating it completely. Place the battered chicken on the wire rack and repeat with the remaining pieces.

4. Let the chicken sit out at room temperature for 20 to 30 minutes before frying.

5. In a large Dutch oven over medium heat, warm about 1 in [2.5 cm] of vegetable oil to 350°F [180°C]. Line a baking sheet with paper towels and set aside.

6. Working in batches, carefully place the chicken in the hot oil, being careful not to crowd the chicken; otherwise, it'll become greasy. Adjust the heat to maintain a consistent 350°F [180°C] temperature.

CONTINUED ⇀

CHOPPIN' AND DIPPIN' FRIED CHICKEN

7. Fry the chicken pieces for 6 to 8 minutes, until golden. Using tongs, carefully turn over each piece and cook for an additional 6 to 8 minutes. If the chicken is getting too dark, lower the heat. When the chicken is done, transfer the pieces to the paper towel–lined baking sheet and sprinkle generously with salt. Repeat with the remaining chicken pieces.

8. Serve the chicken with plenty of hot sauce, if desired.

Smothered Chippin' and Dippin' Fried Chicken

SNOOP

✦ There's something about smothered chicken that does something for me. The fun of watching the oil pop as the chicken fries in the Dutch oven and the smell of fried chicken slowly cooking in a creamy, fragrant broth just takes me back to afternoons in my mama's house, when she'd cook for the family after long days of work. Now I've raised my own kids, and whenever they come by the crib, I like to give them a taste of this good old-fashioned home cooking.

✦

SERVES 6 TO 8

FOR THE CHICKEN

1 lb [455 g] chicken drumsticks and thighs

1 cup [240 ml] buttermilk

1 cup [140 g] all-purpose flour

¾ cups [75 g] crushed Fritos corn chips

1 tsp salt, plus more for seasoning

1 tsp cracked black pepper, plus more for seasoning

½ tsp cayenne pepper

Vegetable oil, for frying

FOR THE GRAVY

3 Tbsp all-purpose flour

¼ tsp onion powder

¼ tsp garlic powder

¼ tsp salt

¼ tsp cracked black pepper

2 cups [480 ml] chicken broth

½ cup [120 ml] whole milk

Cooked white rice or mashed potatoes, for serving

CONTINUED ➝

TO MAKE THE CHICKEN

1. Season the chicken pieces generously with salt and black pepper. In a large bowl, soak the chicken in the buttermilk for at least 15 minutes or up to overnight in the refrigerator.

2. In a large bowl, stir together the flour, crushed corn chips, salt, black pepper, and cayenne until combined. Put the bowl with the buttermilk and chicken next to the flour mixture. Put a wire rack or pan next to the two bowls; this will be where you set your battered chicken.

3. Lift one piece of chicken out of the buttermilk and let any excess drip back into the bowl. Roll the chicken in the flour mixture, coating it completely. Place the battered chicken on the wire rack and repeat with the remaining pieces.

4. Let the chicken sit out at room temperature for 20 to 30 minutes before frying.

5. In a large Dutch oven over medium heat, warm about 1 in [2.5 cm] of vegetable oil to 350°F (180°C). Line a baking sheet with paper towels and set aside.

6. Working in batches, if necessary, to avoid crowding the pan, fry the chicken until brown on both sides, about 6 minutes per side. Transfer the chicken to the prepared baking sheet.

TO MAKE THE GRAVY

1. In a small bowl, combine the flour, onion powder, garlic powder, salt, and pepper.

2. Drain all but ¼ cup [60 ml] of the oil from the Dutch oven.

3. Add the seasoned flour to the Dutch oven and whisk to combine. While whisking, pour in the chicken broth. Let the gravy cook for about 2 minutes, then pour in the milk. Let the gravy cook for about 3 minutes more, then start adding the chicken back into the pan.

4. Cover the pan and let the chicken cook for 30 to 35 minutes, turning the chicken pieces occasionally. Serve the chicken with rice or mashed potatoes.

Mozzarella-Stuffed Turkey Meatloaf with BBQ Sauce

E-40

✦ I know meatloaf doesn't seem like the most gangsta meal on the planet, but in actuality, it's really one of the OGs. Just about every culture has its own version of meatloaf, so I decided to create my own.

✦

**SERVES 4,
WITH LEFTOVERS**

1 lb [455 g] ground turkey

1 lb [455 g] uncased turkey sausage

2 eggs, beaten

½ cup [70 g] bread crumbs

1 medium white onion, chopped

1 red bell pepper, chopped

1 jalapeño, finely chopped

2 garlic cloves, minced

1 tsp salt

½ tsp cracked black pepper

2 cups [160 g] shredded mozzarella

2 cups [475 ml] barbecue sauce, plus more for serving

1. Preheat the oven to 350°F [180°C]. Line a rimmed baking sheet with aluminum foil.

2. In a large bowl, combine the ground turkey, turkey sausage, eggs, bread crumbs, onion, pepper, jalapeño, garlic, salt, and pepper. Combine the mixture well with your hands. Divide the mixture in half.

3. Transfer one half of the mixture to the prepared baking sheet. Form into a 10 in [25 cm] disc about 2 in [5 cm] thick. Pile the shredded mozzarella on top of the disc, spreading it to the edges.

4. Form the remaining turkey into a ball, then flatten it into a disc. Place the disc on top of the mozzarella and pat it so it covers the bottom round of meat. Pour the barbecue sauce on top, spreading it to the edges and over the sides.

5. Bake for 1 to 1½ hours, until cooked through or it measures 160°F [71°C] on a meat thermometer inserted at the thickest part of the loaf. Let cool for 10 minutes before slicing to serve, passing around additional sauce, if desired.

TURKEY MEATLOAF

Magazine Street Special

E-40

No matter what, you gotta remember and pay homage to where you come from. For me, that's Magazine Street in Vallejo, California. I moved there with my mom after she and my dad divorced when I was a kid, and it became our true home. Back then, I spent days hangin' with my friends and cousins, playin' baseball, and choppin' it up with my boys. The neighborhood wasn't perfect, but it was home, and I show love for it whenever I can.

Raising a bunch of kids on the West Coast in the '80s wasn't easy, so my mom really relied on meals that could feed the whole family without spending hours standing over the stove. She came up with her own version of a chicken and rice casserole, hit with vegetables (gotta get ya greens) and flavored with aromatics like celery and onion. Moms taught me well and fed me well too, and now I try to do the same with my own kids. Alright goons, get your aprons and get cooking before I get teary-eyed!

SERVES 4

2 Tbsp butter

1 tsp chopped garlic

1 bunch green onions, thinly sliced

2 cups [140 g] broccoli florets

2 cups [460 g] cooked ground chicken

1 cup [200 g] medium-grain white rice

½ cup [75 g] chopped tomato

½ tsp salt

¼ tsp cracked black pepper

2 cups [475 ml] chicken broth

¼ cup [60 g] sour cream

1 cup [80 g] shredded Havarti cheese

¼ cup [8 g] grated Parmesan cheese

1. Preheat the oven to 425°F [220°C].

2. In a large ovenproof skillet over medium heat, melt the butter. Add the garlic and most of the green onions and cook, stirring occasionally, until softened, 2 minutes. Add the broccoli, chicken, rice, tomato, salt, and pepper. Stir to combine.

3. In a large liquid measuring cup, whisk together the chicken broth and sour cream. Pour into the skillet and bring to a simmer. Stir in the Havarti and Parmesan cheese. Cover with aluminum foil and bake until the rice is tender and most of the liquid is absorbed, about 20 minutes.

4. Remove from the oven, sprinkle with the remaining green onions, and serve.

The Whole Enchilada

E-40

✦ I like to think of enchiladas as a project. Making the sauce and chili beef filling and assembling the ingredients requires some elbow grease, but you've got it, playa. I like to top my enchiladas with jalapeños, but you can dress yours however you'd like.

✦

SERVES 6 TO 8

FOR THE SAUCE

2 medium yellow onions, peeled and quartered

4 garlic cloves, peeled

2 jalapeños

One 28 oz [800 g] can crushed tomatoes

½ tsp ground cumin

½ tsp dried Mexican oregano

½ tsp salt

FOR THE CHILI BEEF FILLING

2 Tbsp vegetable oil

1 small yellow onion, diced

1 garlic clove, minced

1 lb [455 g] ground beef

1 tsp chili powder

Salt and cracked black pepper

15½ oz [440 g] can black, kidney, or pinto beans, drained

FOR ASSEMBLING

8 small flour tortillas

1 lb [455 g] Monterey Jack cheese, grated

Chopped green onions, chopped cilantro, sliced jalapeños, hot sauce, lime wedges, and sour cream, for garnish (optional)

CONTINUED ➙

TO MAKE THE SAUCE

1. Preheat the broiler. Place the onions, garlic, and jalapeños on a baking sheet. Broil until softened and browned, about 10 minutes. Lower the oven heat to 400°F [200°C].

2. Transfer the vegetables to a blender. Add the tomatoes, cumin, oregano, and salt and blend until smooth. Pour the mixture into a medium saucepan over medium heat and simmer until the flavors meld, 5 to 10 minutes. Remove from heat and set aside.

TO MAKE THE CHILI BEEF FILLING

1. Heat a large skillet over medium-high heat. Add the vegetable oil and onions and cook until softened, about 8 minutes. Add the garlic and cook until fragrant, 1 minute. Add the ground beef, breaking it up with a spoon. Add the chili powder, season generously with salt and pepper, and cook until the beef is browned. Add the beans and cook until warmed through. Remove the skillet from the heat and set aside.

TO ASSEMBLE THE ENCHILADAS

1. Place a portion of the beef mixture in a tortilla and roll it up. Place seam-side down in a 9 by 13 in [23 by 33 cm] baking dish and repeat with the remaining beef mixture and tortillas. Pour the sauce on top of the enchiladas. Sprinkle generously with the cheese.

2. Bake until the sauce is bubbling and the cheese is melted and beginning to brown, 20 to 25 minutes. Serve immediately, with the garnishes, if desired.

Uncle Reo's Ribs with BBQ Sauce

SNOOP

My Uncle Reo believed in grilling ribs until the meat falls off the bone, and so do I. This requires patience. Make your BBQ sauce while you give the meat a few hours to cook, and I promise they'll be worth the wait.

SERVES 4

FOR THE RIBS

2 tsp salt

2 tsp cracked black pepper

1 tsp hot paprika

1 tsp chili powder

2 lb [910 g] pork spareribs, membranes removed

FOR THE BBQ SAUCE

1 Tbsp olive oil

¼ cup [35 g] finely diced onion

½ tsp ground cumin

2 Tbsp light brown sugar

3 Tbsp apple cider vinegar

1 Tbsp hot chili sauce

Salt and cracked black pepper, for seasoning

CONTINUED →

TO MAKE THE RIBS

1. Preheat the oven to 275°F [135°C].

2. In a small bowl, combine the salt, pepper, paprika, and chili powder. Season both sides of the ribs with the spice mixture, then place, meat-side up, onto a large rimmed baking sheet.

3. Cover the baking sheet tightly with aluminum foil and bake until the meat falls easily from the bones, 3½ to 4 hours.

TO MAKE THE BBQ SAUCE

1. While the ribs bake, in a medium saucepan over medium heat, warm the olive oil. Add the onion and cook until soft and translucent, 8 minutes. Stir in the cumin and cook for 30 seconds more. Add the sugar, apple cider vinegar, and hot chili sauce. Stir to combine, season with salt and pepper, and cook for 2 minutes more. Set aside.

2. Remove the ribs from the oven, discard the foil, and generously brush both sides of the ribs with the sauce. Serve immediately.

Beef Get Low Mein

SNOOP

✦ I've been lucky to do some big things and make some big bucks in my life, but I remember what it's like to live on a tight budget. And even though I'm in the big leagues now, responsible playas know that every meal doesn't need to break the bank. I love this meal because it's filling, can serve an entire family, and leans on ingredients that are pretty affordable. If you don't have fresh vegetables on hand, frozen works great here, too. Instead of the carrots, bell peppers, shiitake mushrooms, napa cabbage, and snow peas, you can use five cups of frozen stir-fry vegetable mix.

SERVES 4

2 Tbsp soy sauce

2 Tbsp oyster sauce

2 Tbsp Shaoxing rice wine or dry sherry

1 tsp sesame oil

1 tsp brown sugar

½ tsp cracked black pepper

⅛ tsp baking soda

8 oz [230 g] flank steak, cut thinly against the grain into 2 in [5 cm] strips

16 oz [455 g] fresh lo mein noodles or 12 oz [340 g] dried spaghetti or linguine

2 Tbsp vegetable oil

1 medium carrot, julienned

½ red bell pepper, thinly sliced

1 cup [60 g] sliced shiitake mushrooms

3 cups [180 g] thinly sliced napa cabbage

½ cup [50 g] snow peas, strings removed, cut in half

3 green onions, thinly sliced on the diagonal, dark green parts separated

2 garlic cloves, minced

Sriracha, for serving (optional)

1. In a small bowl, whisk together the soy sauce, oyster sauce, rice wine, sesame oil, brown sugar, and black pepper. Transfer 2 Tbsp of the sauce to a medium bowl and whisk in the baking soda. Add the flank steak to the baking soda mixture and toss to coat. Let the beef marinate at room temperature for 15 to 30 minutes.

2. Meanwhile, bring a large pot of water to a boil over high heat. Add the noodles and cook until just tender. Drain in a colander and rinse well under cold water.

3. In a large nonstick skillet over high heat, warm 1 Tbsp of the vegetable oil. Add the beef in a single layer and cook until browned on the first side, 1 to 1½ minutes. Flip the pieces over and cook until browned on the second side, 1½ to 2 minutes more. Transfer to a clean bowl.

4. Add the remaining 1 Tbsp of vegetable oil to the skillet. Add the carrot, bell pepper, and mushrooms and stir-fry until tender-crisp, about 3 minutes. Add the cabbage, snow peas, white and light green parts of the green onions, and garlic. Stir-fry until tender-crisp, about 2 minutes more.

5. Add the noodles, beef, dark green parts of the green onions, and the remaining sauce and toss gently until well mixed and warmed through, about 2 minutes. Serve with sriracha, if desired.

BEEF

GET LOW MEIN

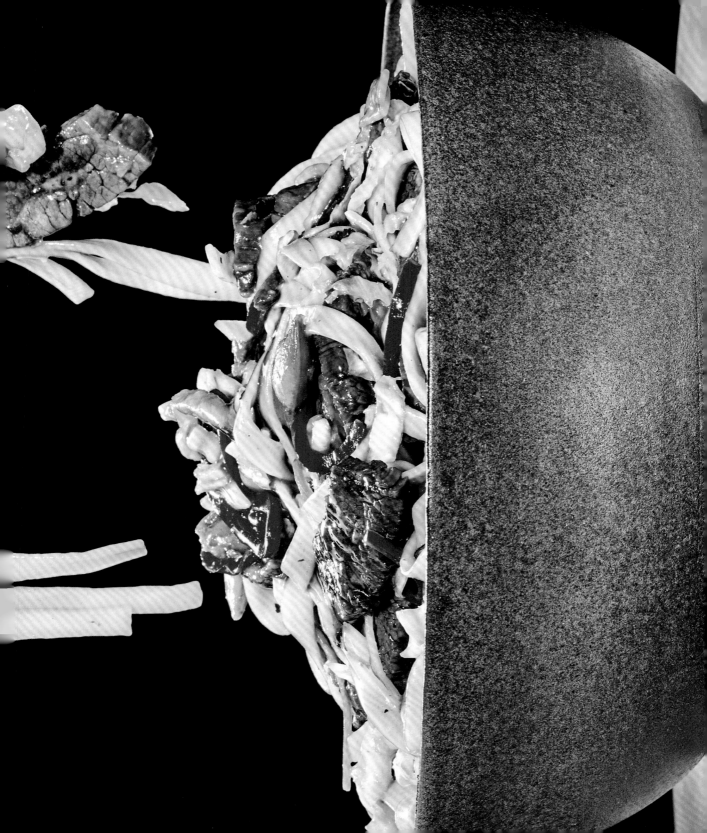

Bacon Cheeseburger Lumpia

E-40

✦ California is a state of flavor, and we get a lot of that flavor from the diverse communities that call this big ol' place home. When I was a kid growing up in Vallejo, I was just as likely to buy a slice of pizza as I was a plate of lumpia—fried Filipino spring rolls that usually come stuffed with vegetables, pork, or some combination of the two. I

✦ love these rolls so much that I now sell them at the Lumpia Company, a lumpia business I co-own with my guy Alex Retodo, one of the best Filipino chefs in the game. Being the Cali boy that I am, I add an American twist to my lumpia, and what's more American than a bacon cheeseburger?

SERVES 8 TO 10

2 Tbsp olive oil

1 cup [140 g] diced onion

5 garlic cloves, minced

1 lb [455 g] 80/20 ground beef

1 cup [180 g] diced maple-cured bacon

2 cups [160 g] finely grated sharp Cheddar cheese

2 tsp cracked black pepper

1 tsp salt

25 square lumpia wrappers, preferably Orientex

Vegetable oil, for frying

1. In a large skillet over medium heat, warm the olive oil. Sauté the onions and garlic until tender, about 8 minutes. Add the beef and bacon and sauté until browned. Add the cheese, stirring to combine. Remove the skillet from the heat and add the pepper and salt.

2. Have a small bowl of water ready. Line a baking sheet with paper towels and set aside.

3. Carefully separate the wrappers. To prevent them from drying out, cover with a damp paper towel. Lay one wrapper on a clean work surface and place 2 to 3 Tbsp of the filling near the edge closest to you. Roll the edge toward the middle, then fold in both sides and continue rolling. Moisten the opposite edge of the wrapper with water to seal. Repeat with the remaining filling and wrappers.

4. In a large Dutch oven over medium heat, warm about 1 in [2.5 cm] of vegetable oil to 350°F [180°C]. Add the lumpia and fry until golden brown, 3 to 5 minutes, flipping once. When done, use a slotted spoon to transfer the lumpia to the prepared baking sheet to drain. Serve immediately.

THE ULTIMATE COOKOUT:
Burgers & Doggs

Americans in every single part of this country know the power of a good ass cookout. A cookout is more than just a time to eat some grub; it's a time to eat the most nostalgic food with the friends and family you love the most and feel most yourself with. It's a sacred space for us, filled with kids dancin' to the Wobble, uncles playing spades, and somebody who ain't even bring anything trying to take five different plates of to-go food. It's wild, it's fun, and it's us—and that's what we all love about it!

Unsurprisingly, there are some rules to the cookout. Only experienced aunties can do the mac 'n' cheese, uncles who wear those brown fisherman sandals (don't act like you don't know the ones we're talkin' about) probably got the best skills on the grill, and please, please don't eat the potato salad if you don't know who made it (and don't say we ain't warn you if you do!). Now, we like to throw a cookout every now and then, and for our families, that means we've got to keep the hamburgers and hot dogs coming. These are doable even for beginners on the grill, and the banana ketchup is going to impress even the most old school pitmasters at the party.

SERVES 8 TO 12

FOR THE BURGERS

1 lb [455 g] ground beef

1 Tbsp olive oil

1 Tbsp Worcestershire sauce

1 tsp salt

½ tsp garlic powder

FOR THE HOT DOGS

8 hot dogs

Barbecue sauce, for brushing

FOR SERVING

4 hamburger buns

8 hot dog buns

Sliced cheese, sliced onions, lettuce, Banana Ketchup (page 140), mustard, relish, diced onions, and pickled jalapeños, for topping (optional)

TO MAKE THE BURGERS

1. Preheat a grill to medium-high heat.

2. Place the beef, olive oil, Worcestershire sauce, salt, and garlic powder in a large bowl. Use your hands to mix the ingredients together until just combined, being careful not to overwork the meat.

3. Shape the meat into ½ in [13 mm] thick patties, about 4 oz [115 g] each. Press your thumb into the center of each patty to make an indentation; this will keep the burgers from bulging out when cooking.

4. Cook the patties for 4 to 5 minutes with the grill lid closed, until they are browned on the bottom and the only juices visible are no longer red. Do not push down on the patties or move them around while cooking. Flip the patties over and cook for 2 to 3 minutes more for medium, or until done as desired. Remove the burgers from the heat and let rest for a few minutes before serving.

TO MAKE THE HOT DOGS

Grill the hot dogs, turning them occasionally, until lightly charred in spots, 5 to 7 minutes. Brush the hot dogs with barbecue sauce during the last minute of cooking.

TO SERVE

Toast the buns on the grill for about 30 seconds. Serve the hamburgers and hot dogs on the buns and add any desired toppings.

THE ULTIMATE COOKOUT: BURGERS & DOGS

THE ULTIMATE COOKOUT:
Banana Ketchup

Don't let the ingredient list scare you. Once you've gathered everything you need, this stovetop ketchup comes together in about ten minutes. Plus, you can keep leftovers in the fridge for a couple of weeks. Use them on another hot dog or burger or for dipping anything you can think of (hint: lumpia, Man-ish Sandwich [page 73], fried wontons, or French fries).

MAKES 2 CUPS [480 G]

2 Tbsp vegetable oil

½ cup [70 g] finely chopped yellow onion

1 jalapeño, stemmed, seeded, and minced

1 Tbsp minced fresh ginger

1 tsp minced garlic

½ tsp ground turmeric

¼ tsp ground allspice

2 Tbsp tomato paste

2 cups [600 g] mashed ripe bananas

½ cup [100 g] packed light brown sugar

½ cup [120 ml] white wine vinegar

2 Tbsp soy sauce

2 Tbsp dark rum (optional)

1. In a small saucepan over medium heat, warm the vegetable oil. Add the onion and cook, stirring, until softened, about 5 minutes. Stir in the jalapeño, ginger, garlic, turmeric, and allspice and cook, stirring, until fragrant, about 1 minute. Add the tomato paste and cook, stirring, until lightly caramelized, about 1 minute.

2. Add the mashed bananas, brown sugar, vinegar, soy sauce, and rum, if using, and simmer, stirring occasionally, until slightly thickened, about 10 minutes. Scrape the sauce into a bowl, press a sheet of plastic wrap against the surface of the ketchup, and let cool. Store in an airtight container in the refrigerator for up to 2 weeks.

THE ULTIMATE COOKOUT:
Fried Plantains

We can't thank the Caribbean region enough for giving the world plantains. There are so many ways to enjoy this special type of banana: boiled, mashed, and even roasted. But for a cookout? Fried is the way to go.

SERVES 2

2 ripe plantains

Vegetable oil, for frying

Salt

1. Cut the ends off the plantains and slice along the length of the plantains to remove the peels. Slice the plantains crosswise into ½ in [13 mm] rounds.

2. In a large skillet over medium-high heat, heat about ⅛ in [3 mm] of vegetable oil until it shimmers. Line a plate with paper towels and set aside.

3. Working in batches, carefully add the plantain rounds to the hot oil, being careful not to crowd them. Fry the plantains for 2 to 3 minutes per side, until golden brown. When done, transfer to the prepared plate. Sprinkle generously with salt and serve warm.

Short Rib Adobo

E-40

✦ Los Angeles is home to the largest population of Filipinos in the United States, and Filipino cuisine is a huge part of California's foodways. I'm grateful for it. Some of my best friends—and best meals—come from the Filipino community, and I've been lucky enough to learn from them. One of the things the community put me onto is adobo, which is basically immersing cooked food in a mixture of vinegar and various spices, aromatics, and salt. At home, I like to do a short rib adobo, which I serve with mashed potatoes and white rice. Like barbecued ribs, the key here is patience. Give the meat time to cook so you get the tender texture. And watch those Thai chiles! Even for a G like me, they can pack some heat.

SERVES 4

3 Tbsp vegetable oil

4 (4 lb [1.8 kg]) bone-in beef short ribs

1 tsp salt

1 tsp cracked black pepper

1 cup [240 ml] chicken broth

1 cup [240 ml] unsweetened coconut milk

¾ cup [180 ml] sherry vinegar

¾ cup [180 ml] light soy sauce

12 garlic cloves, peeled

3 bay leaves

1 small red Thai chile

Mashed potatoes or cooked white rice, for serving

Cilantro sprigs, for garnish (optional)

1. In a large saucepan over medium-high heat, warm the vegetable oil. Season the ribs with the salt and pepper. Working in batches, add the ribs to the pan and cook, turning as needed, until the ribs are browned, about 15 minutes. Remove the ribs from the pan.

2. Pour out and discard all but 2 Tbsp of the oil from the pan and return to the heat. Stir in the broth, coconut milk, vinegar, soy sauce, garlic, bay leaves, and chile and bring the mixture to a boil. Add the ribs back to the pan, lower the heat to medium-low, cover, and cook, stirring occasionally, until the meat is falling off the bones, 2½ to 3 hours.

3. Transfer the ribs to a serving platter and cover to keep warm. Simmer the sauce over medium-high heat until thickened, 18 to 20 minutes. Discard the garlic, bay leaves, and Thai chile. Pour the sauce over the ribs and serve with mashed potatoes or white rice, garnishing with cilantro sprigs, if desired.

CHAPTER 5

SIDES

Shrimp Salad [146]

Chicken Wing Salad [148]

Kickin' Lickin' Collard Greens [153]

Roasted Karats [154]

Cognac Mashed Potatoes [156]

Cornbread Rice [159]

Easy Cheesy Garlic Bread [160]

Shrimp Salad

SNOOP

I love shrimp, and this appetizer gives me a great chance to highlight this little crustacean. I serve my shrimp salad on crackers at parties, because it's so easy to make but looks beautiful on a serving platter. Gotta shout out my Maryland peeps too: Y'all really snapped with Old Bay Seasoning, and it's essential to get this salad just right.

SERVES 4 TO 6

2 Tbsp plus ¾ tsp Old Bay seasoning

1 lb [455 g] 21/25-count shrimp, peeled and deveined

½ cup [120 g] mayonnaise

1 Tbsp chopped fresh dill, plus additional fronds for garnish

2 tsp fresh lemon juice

2 tsp Dijon mustard

¼ tsp cracked black pepper

1 shallot, finely diced

½ cup [60 g] finely diced celery

½ cup [60 g] finely diced red bell pepper

Buttery crackers, bagel chips, or melba toasts, for serving

1. In a large saucepan over medium-high heat, bring 6 cups [1.4 L] of water and 2 Tbsp of the Old Bay to a boil. Add the shrimp and simmer, uncovered, until the shrimp are firm and opaque all the way through, about 2 minutes.

2. Drain in a colander and transfer the shrimp to a large bowl of ice water. When the shrimp have cooled completely, drain again in the colander and pat dry with paper towels. Chop the shrimp into ½ in [13 mm] pieces.

3. In a medium bowl, whisk together the mayonnaise, dill, lemon juice, Dijon, pepper, and remaining ¾ tsp of Old Bay. Add the shrimp, shallot, celery, and bell pepper and stir to combine.

4. Transfer to a serving bowl and garnish with additional dill fronds. Serve on top of crackers.

Chicken Wing Salad

E-40

✦ I love chicken wings, but I'm also thinking about nutrition a bit more than I was twenty years ago. Hey, I gotta set an example for the kids, man! Cali has some of the best produce on the planet, so I love using fruits and vegetables like mandarins, mixed greens, and napa cabbage. Use whatever's in season where you are, and don't forget the lemon pepper! It adds an extra layer of flavor that really sets this salad off.

SERVES 4

FOR THE VINAIGRETTE

⅓ cup [80 ml] vegetable oil

¼ cup [60 ml] rice vinegar

1 Tbsp honey

1 tsp toasted sesame oil

½ tsp salt

FOR THE BRINE

⅓ cup [65 g] sugar

⅓ cup [55 g] salt

1 bay leaf

1 tsp red pepper flakes

Peel of 1 orange

FOR THE CHICKEN

1 lb [455 g] boneless chicken tenders (8 pieces)

1 cup [140 g] all-purpose flour

¼ cup [14 g] crushed potato chips

1 tsp garlic powder

1 tsp baking powder

1 tsp salt, plus more for seasoning

1 tsp cracked black pepper

½ cup [120 ml] buttermilk

Vegetable oil, for frying

Lemon pepper seasoning (optional)

FOR THE SALAD

3 cups [180 g] thinly sliced napa cabbage

6 cups [140 g] loosely packed mixed greens

2 navel oranges, peeled and cut into individual segments, or one 15 oz [425 g] can mandarin orange segments, drained

1 green onion, thinly sliced

¼ cup [5 g] fresh cilantro leaves

¼ cup [25 g] toasted sliced almonds

¼ cup [10 g] fried wonton strips

CONTINUED ➙

TO MAKE THE VINAIGRETTE

In a small bowl or jar with a lid, combine the vegetable oil, vinegar, honey, sesame oil, and salt. Whisk, or cover the jar and shake vigorously, until combined. Set aside.

TO BRINE THE CHICKEN

1. Fill a large pot with 5 cups [1.2 L] of water. Place the pot over high heat and bring to a boil. Add the sugar, salt, bay leaf, red pepper flakes, and orange peel. Cook, stirring, until the sugar and salt dissolve, about 1 minute. Remove from the heat and let cool to room temperature.

2. Place the chicken in a large bowl and cover completely with the cooled brine. Cover and refrigerate for at least 10 hours and up to 24 hours.

3. Remove the chicken from the brine and pat the pieces dry with a paper towel. Set the chicken aside and discard the brine.

TO BATTER THE CHICKEN

1. In a large bowl, stir together the flour, crushed potato chips, garlic powder, baking powder, salt, and black pepper until combined. Transfer the mixture to a large, shallow dish. Put a medium bowl next to the flour mixture and pour in the buttermilk. Put a wire rack next to the two dishes.

2. Take one chicken tender and submerge it in the buttermilk, allowing any excess to drip back into the bowl. Roll the tender in the flour mixture, coating it completely. Place the battered chicken on the wire rack and repeat with the remaining tenders.

3. Let the tenders sit at room temperature for 20 to 30 minutes before frying.

TO FRY THE CHICKEN

1. In a large Dutch oven over medium heat, warm about 1 in [2.5 cm] of vegetable oil to 350°F [180°C]. Line a baking sheet with paper towels and set aside.

2. Working in batches, carefully place the chicken in the hot oil. Adjust the heat to maintain a consistent 350°F [180°C] temperature.

3. Fry the tenders until golden, 8 to 10 minutes, flipping halfway through so they brown evenly. Remove each piece with tongs and transfer it to the paper towel–lined baking sheet. Sprinkle generously with salt or lemon pepper, if using. Repeat with the remaining chicken.

TO MAKE THE SALAD

1. In a large bowl, toss the cabbage, greens, orange pieces, green onion, cilantro, and almonds until combined. Add ½ cup [120 ml] of the vinaigrette and toss until evenly coated. Slice the fried chicken tenders.

2. Divide the salad among four individual bowls and top with the fried wonton strips and chicken tenders. Drizzle with additional vinaigrette, if desired.

Kickin' Lickin' Collard Greens

E-40

◆ Like a lot of Black folks from the Bay Area, my family originally comes from the Deep South. I've got family from places like Louisiana and Mississippi, which is where my dad grew up, and some of Snoop's family too. Our ancestors in the South brought so many culinary traditions from West Africa and created so many dishes that we love and claim as American, like mac 'n' cheese, sweet potato pie (I know somebody got an auntie who knows how to throw down during the holidays), and one of my favorites, collard greens. When I make my collards, I often think about my ancestors and the sacrifices they made to make sure our community had food and culture that we could call our own. I also think about how recipes change and evolve over time. Like many collard green recipes, mine is flavored with pork—ham steak, to be exact—and I hit my greens with red pepper flakes and Crystal hot sauce to make 'em extra kickin' and lickin'. Don't forget, playas: Like my momma always said, before you start cooking, wash those collard greens well! You don't want no dirt or sand messin' up your pot of goodness.

SERVES 6 TO 8

1 tsp olive oil

2 slices bacon, cut crosswise into ½ in [13 mm] pieces

1 medium sweet onion, halved and thinly sliced

3 garlic cloves, minced

¼ tsp red pepper flakes

4 oz [115 g] ham steak, cut into ½ in [13 mm] dice (about 1 cup)

3 cups [710 ml] low-sodium chicken broth

2 lb [910 g] collard greens, stems removed, leaves cut into ½ in [13 mm] ribbons

2 tsp apple cider vinegar

Salt and cracked black pepper

Hot sauce, preferably Crystal, for serving

1. In a Dutch oven or large pot over medium heat, warm the olive oil. Add the bacon and cook until just starting to crisp, 3 to 4 minutes.

2. Add the onion and cook, stirring occasionally, until golden brown and starting to soften, about 6 minutes. Add the garlic and red pepper flakes and cook until fragrant, about 1 minute. Stir in the ham.

3. Add the broth and collard greens, increase the heat to medium-high, and bring to a boil. Lower the heat to medium-low and cook, uncovered, until the greens are very tender, about 30 minutes, stirring occasionally.

4. Stir in the vinegar and season with salt and black pepper. Serve immediately, seasoning individual servings with hot sauce.

Roasted Karats

✦ There's a lot to love about living in the Golden State, and produce has to be in the top five. California has some of the freshest, most seasonal cooking in the country. People come from far and wide just to get a bit of our fruits and vegetables, like artichokes, plums, and avocados. Carrots, which are in season during the spring and fall, are so easy to cook with. I like my citrus and acid; I like to coat my roasted carrots with lime juice. Give it a try. You won't be disappointed.

SERVES 4

1 Tbsp vegetable oil

1 Tbsp fish sauce

1 Tbsp honey

½ tsp grated fresh ginger

¼ tsp cracked black pepper

1 garlic clove, minced

1 lb [455 g] medium carrots, peeled and halved lengthwise

1 tsp fresh lime juice

½ tsp finely grated lime zest

Chopped parsley, for garnish (optional)

1. Preheat the oven to 500°F [260°C]. Line a baking sheet with aluminum foil and place it in the oven.

2. In a medium bowl, whisk together the vegetable oil, fish sauce, honey, ginger, pepper, and garlic until combined. Add the carrots and toss until well coated. Reserve the bowl for later use (do not wash).

3. Transfer the carrots to the prepared baking sheet and spread them in an even layer. Roast until the carrots start to brown on the bottom, 8 to 10 minutes. Stir the carrots and continue to roast until tender and browned, 4 to 5 minutes more.

4. Return the carrots to the bowl and add the lime juice and zest; toss to coat. Transfer to a serving bowl, garnish with parsley, if desired, and serve immediately.

Cognac Mashed Potatoes

SNOOP

◆ These ain't ya mama's mashed potatoes, y'all! Now, I gave y'all a recipe for mash in my first cookbook, *From Crook to Cook*. But guess what, goons? I'm feeling ultra-generous, so I'm hooking you up with my other favorite way to eat this Thanksgiving staple: laced with cognac. Now, I know what you're thinking. Isn't cognac more for a concert with the Dogg rather than Thanksgiving with the Dogg? My answer to that?
◆ Why not both?! Infusing cognac into the butter and cream mixture adds spice, a bit of sweetness, and depth to the flavor, not to mention transforms the texture into an even creamier batch of potatoes. Get that potato masher ready, and get ready to stun your relatives at the holidays.

SERVES 6 TO 8

Salt

4 lb [1.8 kg] russet potatoes, cut into chunks

4 Tbsp [55 g] unsalted butter

2 cups [480 ml] heavy cream

½ cup [120 g] mayonnaise

½ cup [120 ml] cognac or brandy

Cracked black pepper

1. Bring a large pot of heavily salted water to a boil over high heat. Lower the heat to medium-high and add the potatoes. Cook until tender, about 25 minutes. Drain and set aside, covered.

2. Return the empty pot to medium heat and melt the butter. Add the cream, mayonnaise, and cognac. Whisk until combined and warmed through.

3. Return the potatoes to the pot. Using a potato masher, mash to combine with the cream mixture. Season with salt and pepper as needed. Serve immediately.

Cornbread Rice

✦   What is cornbread rice? Make it and find out.

SNOOP

✦

SERVES 6 TO 8

1 tsp vegetable oil

8 oz [230 g] sweet Italian sausage, casings removed

3 Tbsp unsalted butter

1 medium sweet onion, diced

1 green bell pepper, diced

1 cup [120 g] diced celery

3 garlic cloves, minced

2 Tbsp finely chopped fresh sage

1 tsp Creole seasoning

2 cups [480 ml] low-sodium chicken broth

1 lb [455 g] cornbread, broken into ½ in [13 mm] crumbles (about 5 cups)

2 cups [240 g] cooked long-grain rice, cooled

2 eggs, lightly beaten

1. Preheat the oven to 350°F [180°C]. Grease a 9 by 9 in [23 by 23 cm] square baking dish.

2. In a large skillet over medium-high heat, warm the vegetable oil. Add the sausage and cook until well browned, 8 to 10 minutes, using a spatula to break up the meat into small pieces. Transfer to a bowl and set aside.

3. Turn down the heat to medium and melt the butter. Add the onion, bell pepper, and celery and cook until tender, 8 to 10 minutes, stirring occasionally. Add the garlic, sage, and Creole seasoning and cook until fragrant, about 1 minute. Return the sausage to the skillet, add the chicken broth, increase the heat to medium-high, and bring to a simmer.

4. In a large bowl, combine the cornbread, rice, and eggs. Fold in the sausage mixture, then transfer to the prepared baking dish. Bake until the top is golden brown, about 30 minutes. Let cool for 5 minutes before serving.

Easy Cheesy Garlic Bread

E-40

I always make sure to get some of the things I love from the Lone Star State, like enchiladas, tacos, burritos, barbecue, and Texas toast, which is thicker than your average slice of toast. That thick piece of bread absorbs generous amounts of butter and garlic that elevates just about any sandwich. I love this toast so much, I had to create my own version. Like they say, everything is bigger in Texas, so use this toast for your biggest, baddest days when you're feeling extra ravenous.

SERVES 6 TO 8

6 Tbsp [85 g] unsalted butter

3 garlic cloves, minced

½ cup [15 g] grated Parmesan

½ tsp garlic powder

¼ tsp salt

Pinch of red pepper flakes

1 Tbsp chopped parsley (optional)

1 baguette or thin Italian bread loaf

8 slices provolone

1. Preheat the oven to 400°F [200°C]. Lay a large rectangle of aluminum foil on a rimmed baking sheet.

2. In a small pan over medium-low heat, melt the butter with the garlic. Remove from the heat and stir in the Parmesan, garlic powder, salt, red pepper flakes, and parsley, if using.

3. Cut the bread in half lengthwise and place the two halves on the foil cut-side up. Divide the butter mixture evenly between the halves, spreading it into the bread. Press the halves together and wrap in the foil. Place the wrapped loaf on the baking sheet and bake for 5 minutes.

4. Remove the baking sheet from the oven, unwrap the foil, and place the two halves buttered-side up back on the baking sheet. Bake until lightly toasted, about 5 minutes.

5. Remove the sheet from the oven and cover each bread half with provolone slices. Bake until the cheese is melted, about 5 minutes.

6. Slice the bread into 2 in [5 cm] segments and serve immediately.

CHAPTER 6

SWEETS

PB Cookie
Ice Cream Sammies [164]

Corner Store Slushies [167]

Purple Popsizzles [168]

Grilled Peaches 'n' Cream [170]

Wiggle Wiggle Fruit Squares [173]

Green Brownies [175]

Snoop's Fruity Loop Bars [178]

Snickers Pocket Pastries [181]

Banana Lumpia with Caramel [183]

Leche Flan [184]

PB Cookie Ice Cream Sammies

SNOOP

I love a good, cold sweet treat on a hot summer day. In the summer, when I'm craving my Rolls Royce PB–Chocolate Chip Cookie from my first cookbook, *From Crook to Cook*, I take out the chips and turn the cookie into an ice cream sandwich. I could pretend that I do this for my grandkids, but y'all know the D.O. Double G has a sweet tooth. I own it!

MAKES 12 SANDWICHES

2½ cups [350 g] all-purpose flour

¾ tsp baking powder

½ tsp baking soda

¼ tsp salt

2 cups (4 sticks [455 g]) unsalted butter, at room temperature

1 cup [260 g] creamy peanut butter

2 cups [400 g] granulated sugar

1 cup [200 g] packed light brown sugar

2 eggs

1 tsp vanilla extract

2 pints [960 g] vanilla or chocolate ice cream, for serving

Sprinkles or crushed peanuts, for garnish (optional)

1. Preheat the oven to 350°F [180°C]. Line two baking sheets with parchment paper.

2. In a small bowl, stir together the flour, baking powder, baking soda, and salt.

3. In a large bowl or the bowl of a stand mixer, combine the butter, peanut butter, 1 cup [200 g] of the granulated sugar, and the brown sugar. Beat on medium speed until creamy and smooth. Add the eggs and vanilla, beating until combined, then reduce the mixer speed to low, add the flour mixture, and beat until just combined. Cover the mixture and refrigerate for at least 1 hour and up to 2 days.

4. Pour the remaining 1 cup [200 g] of granulated sugar into a shallow bowl. Using a small scoop, scoop the dough and form 24 balls. Roll each ball in the sugar to coat, then place the balls on the prepared baking sheets, spacing them at least 2 in [5 cm] apart. Use the tines of a fork to press down on each ball and create the traditional crisscross pattern.

5. Bake until the edges of the cookies are golden, 10 to 12 minutes. Do not overbake, as these should be chewy; they will firm up as they cool. Transfer the cookies to a wire rack and cool completely.

6. Before assembling, let the ice cream sit out for 15 minutes to soften. Turn 12 cookies flat-side up. Top each with a generous scoop of ice cream and place another cookie on top. Push down to squish the ice cream to the edges of the cookies. Roll the exposed ice cream sides in the sprinkles, if using. Wrap each cookie sandwich in plastic wrap and freeze for at least 2 hours and up to 2 weeks.

Corner Store Slushies

E-40

Don't sleep on the corner store. Candy, chips, hot dogs—all the good grub a young gangsta like me needed back in the day. I'm not at corner stores as much as I used to be when I was a teenager, but I still crave those Slurpees that they'd sell for $0.99. I know everybody from Houston to New York to Atlanta got a corner store that they have fond memories about, and this Slurpee brings a bit of that nostalgia to your kitchen.

For a swirl, try making this by adding half Cherry and half Tropical Punch Kool-Aid Drink Mix powder to a glass and gently blend them together. And for all my grown folks, get the boozy party started by adding an ounce [30 ml] of your favorite shot of alcohol on top.

MAKES 3 CUPS [710 ML]

½ cup [100 g] sugar

3 Tbsp Kool-Aid Drink Mix powder (Cherry or Tropical Punch)

16 oz [480 ml] club soda

3 cups [400 g] ice cubes

Maraschino cherries, for garnish

1. In a blender, add the sugar, Kool-Aid Drink Mix, club soda, and ice. Blend on high speed until the mixture has a slushy consistency, 30 to 45 seconds.

2. Pour into serving glasses and top with a maraschino cherry. Serve immediately.

Purple Popsizzles

SNOOP

✦ These boozy popsicles get their color from a blend of hibiscus tea and grape juice. It's rare to enjoy a popsicle that looks and smells good, but you know the D.O. Double G is an innovator at heart!

✦

MAKES 6 TO 8 POPS

2 hibiscus tea bags

2 Tbsp sugar

¾ cup [180 ml] purple grape juice

2 Tbsp bourbon, rye whiskey, or gin (optional)

1 Tbsp fresh lemon juice

1. Make some space in your freezer for your pops. Set out your molds or Dixie cups and sticks.

2. In a small saucepan, bring 1 cup [240 ml] of water to a boil. Remove from the heat, add the tea bags and sugar, and let stand for 10 minutes. Discard the tea bags, then stir to dissolve the sugar.

3. Let the liquid cool completely, about 30 minutes (you can place it in the refrigerator to speed this up). Once cool, stir in the grape juice, bourbon (if using), and lemon juice.

4. Pour the mixture into ice-pop molds and insert popsicle sticks. Freeze until firm, at least 6 hours.

5. To unmold the pops, run hot water over the outside of the molds for a few seconds, then gently tug. If you used Dixie cups, rip and peel away the paper cup. Eat immediately, or freeze for up to 1 week.

Grilled Peaches 'n' Cream

E-40 + SNOOP

✦ Meat ain't the only thing you can fire up on the grill. Putting fruit on the grill can give your produce a smoky flavor, not to mention add texture and body to a dish. After enjoying some burgers and hot dogs during summer barbecues, we like to give our families this creamy dessert. The cream breaks down the acidity of the peaches, and the honey and bourbon ramp up the rich, sweet flavors.

SERVES 4

FOR THE BOURBON WHIPPED CREAM

½ cup [120 ml] heavy cream

2 tsp bourbon

½ tsp vanilla extract

1 Tbsp sugar

¼ tsp ground cinnamon

FOR THE PEACHES

2 large, firm yet ripe peaches, halved and pitted

Vegetable oil, for brushing

2 tsp honey

2 Tbsp toasted chopped pecans

TO MAKE THE BOURBON WHIPPED CREAM

1. Refrigerate the bowl of a stand mixer and the whisk attachment, or a medium metal bowl and the beaters of a handheld electric mixer, for about 15 minutes, until quite cold.

2. Once chilled, remove the bowl and whisk from the refrigerator. Add the cream and whip on medium speed until just thickened.

3. Add the bourbon, vanilla, sugar, and cinnamon. Whip on medium-high speed until the cream holds soft peaks. Refrigerate until ready to use.

TO MAKE THE PEACHES

1. Preheat an outdoor grill or indoor grill pan over medium-high heat. Lightly brush the cut sides of the peaches with vegetable oil and lightly oil the grill grates or grill pan.

2. Grill the peach halves cut-side down until tender and dark brown grill marks appear, 2 to 4 minutes. Transfer the peaches cut-side up to individual plates, drizzle with the honey, and let cool slightly.

3. Top each peach half with a dollop of whipped cream and sprinkle with chopped pecans.

Wiggle Wiggle Fruit Squares

SNOOP

✦ Wiggle it, jiggle it, friends! That's how I keep it moving with my strawberry fruit squares. I took the old-school Jell-O fruit salad and gave it a twenty-first-century look. This sliceable treat has a buttery crust, sweet cream cheese filling, and strawberry Jell-O topping that wiggles and jiggles.

✦

SERVES 8 TO 10

FOR THE CRUST

4½ cups [170 g] salted pretzel twists

2 Tbsp sugar

12 Tbsp (1½ sticks [170 g]) unsalted butter, melted

FOR THE CREAM CHEESE FILLING

4 oz [115 g] cream cheese, at room temperature

⅓ cup [65 g] sugar

1 tsp vanilla extract

1 cup [70 g] whipped topping, preferably Cool Whip

FOR THE GELATIN LAYER

One 6 oz [170 g] package strawberry-flavored gelatin, preferably Jell-O

2 cups [480 ml] boiling water

2 cups [230 g] sliced frozen strawberries

Whipped topping and sliced fresh strawberries, for serving (optional)

CONTINUED ➡

TO MAKE THE CRUST

1. Preheat the oven to 350°F [180°C]. Spray an 8 by 8 in [20 by 20 cm] baking pan with nonstick cooking spray.

2. Place the pretzels and sugar in the bowl of a food processor and process until finely ground. Add the butter and pulse until the mixture looks like wet sand and begins to clump together. Pour the mixture into the prepared pan and press into an even and compact layer. Bake the crust until golden brown and set, about 10 minutes. Place on a wire rack to cool completely.

TO MAKE THE CREAM CHEESE FILLING

1. Place the cream cheese, sugar, and vanilla in the bowl of a stand mixer fitted with the paddle attachment and beat on medium speed until fluffy, about 2 minutes, stopping to scrape down the sides and bottom of the bowl with a spatula as needed.

2. Gently fold in the whipped topping with the spatula until combined. Spread the filling evenly over the cooled pretzel crust. Refrigerate until ready to use.

TO MAKE THE GELATIN LAYER AND ASSEMBLE

1. In a large bowl, stir together the gelatin and boiling water until dissolved. Stir in the strawberries and refrigerate until partially set, 30 to 45 minutes.

2. Gently spread the gelatin mixture over the cream cheese filling. Refrigerate until completely set, at least 2 hours and up to 24 hours.

3. To serve, cut into squares and top with additional whipped topping and sliced strawberries, if desired.

Green Brownies

No, not that kind of green brownies—though, we aren't opposed to those, either! Get a green mint ice cream to serve over this very minty brownie dish, which gets a double dose of flavor thanks to melted chocolate mint candies baked into the base and whole chocolate peppermint patties distributed throughout.

MAKES 9 BROWNIES

¾ cup [105 g] all-purpose flour

½ tsp salt

¼ tsp baking soda

½ cup [80 g] chopped chocolate mints, preferably Andes chocolate mints

½ cup [40 g] cocoa powder

¾ cup [150 g] sugar

6 Tbsp [90 ml] vegetable oil

2 eggs, lightly beaten

16 chocolate-covered peppermint patties, preferably York Peppermint Patties

Mint chocolate chip ice cream, for serving

CONTINUED ➜

1. Preheat the oven to 325°F [165°C]. Grease an 8 by 8 in [20 by 20 cm] baking pan and set aside.

2. In a small bowl, whisk together the flour, salt, and baking soda. Set aside.

3. In a medium saucepan over medium-high heat, bring ⅓ cup [80 ml] of water to a boil. Remove the pan from the heat and add the chocolate mints and cocoa powder. Stir until the chocolate is melted and smooth. Transfer to a medium bowl.

4. Add the sugar, vegetable oil, and eggs to the chocolate mixture. Stir until blended and smooth.

5. Gradually add the flour mixture to the chocolate mixture, stirring until just combined. Spread half of the batter evenly into the prepared pan, then arrange the peppermint patties evenly on top. Gently spread the remaining batter on top of the patties.

6. Bake until the top and edges are set and a toothpick inserted into an area away from the peppermint patties comes out with a few moist crumbs attached, 25 to 30 minutes, rotating the pan halfway through baking.

7. Place the pan on a wire rack and let cool for 1 hour. Invert the brownies onto the rack and let cool completely.

8. Invert the brownies onto a cutting board and cut into nine pieces. Serve topped with a scoop of mint chocolate chip ice cream.

Snoop's Fruity Loop Bars

✦ Ladies and gentlemen, I present to you: Snoop Loops! That's right, scrubs. If y'all remember anything from my first cookbook, you remember that I love me some breakfast cereal, especially Fruit Loops. Instead of dropping these colorful loops in a bowl of milk, I gave them the marshmallow bar treatment.

✦

MAKES 24 BARS

6 Tbsp [85 g] salted butter

One 1 lb [455 g] bag
of marshmallows

2 tsp vanilla extract

4 cups [100 g] crisped rice
cereal

2 cups [60 g] Fruit Loops or
other fruit cereal

1 cup [180 g] white
chocolate chips

1. Tear a sheet of aluminum foil large enough to line a 9 by 13 in [23 by 33 cm] baking pan with a 4 in [10 cm] overhang on opposite ends. Butter the foil generously and press it into the pan, smoothing down the sides. Reserve the butter wrapper.

2. In a large pot over medium heat, melt the butter. Add the marshmallows and stir until melted and smooth. Remove the pot from the heat and add the vanilla.

3. Using a rubber or silicone spatula, and working quickly, mix the crisped rice cereal, fruit cereal, and white chocolate chips into the marshmallow mixture. Turn the mixture out into the prepared pan. Use the reserved butter wrapper to firmly press the mixture into an even layer, filling the pan. Let the mixture sit at room temperature until cool.

4. Use the foil overhang to lift the slab of treats onto a cutting board. Cut into 24 pieces. Store in an airtight container at room temperature for up to 3 days.

Snickers Pocket Pastries

E-40

✦ I apologize to the parents in advance: Yes, your kids will be asking for this every day, getting their sugar on early in the a.m. Life isn't supposed to be dull, fam. Brighten your life with one of the sweetest treats I cook in my kitchen, stuffed with the best chocolate candy on the planet. And look, who says candy is just for the kiddos?

MAKES 6 TARTS

1 egg

One 15.1 oz [430 g] package refrigerated pie crust (two pie crusts)

12 mini Snickers candies

Chocolate sprinkles

1. Preheat the oven to 400°F [200°C]. Line a baking sheet with parchment paper and set aside.

2. Whisk together the egg and 1 tsp of water in a small bowl until combined. Set aside.

3. Flour a large work surface and lay out both pie crusts. Roll the dough into 11 in [28 cm] circles and use a knife or pizza cutter to trim the edges, about 1 in [2.5 cm] off all sides, to create two 9 in [23 cm] squares. Cut each square into six 3 by 4½ in [7.5 by 11 cm] rectangles (twelve total).

4. Place two Snickers candies each in the middle of six of the rectangles, then brush the egg wash around the Snickers. Place an empty dough rectangle over a Snickers-filled rectangle and use a fork to crimp the edges of the dough together on all sides. Repeat with the remaining dough rectangles. Brush the tops with the remaining egg wash and sprinkle with chocolate sprinkles.

5. Place the pastries on the prepared baking sheet and bake for 18 to 20 minutes, until golden. Transfer the pastries to a wire rack to cool.

6. Serve warm. Leftover tarts will keep in an airtight container at room temperature for 2 to 3 days.

Banana Lumpia with Caramel

E-40

✦ Lumpia doesn't have to be savory. I realized that banana and caramel might be a good match for the fried rolls. These vegan-friendly dessert rolls showcase the many possibilities of lumpia in the sweetest way possible.

✦

SERVES 6 TO 8

FOR THE SAUCE

1 cup [240 ml] coconut milk

¾ cup [150 g] packed dark brown sugar

FOR THE LUMPIA

½ cup [100 g] packed light brown sugar

6 bananas or plantains, halved

12 lumpia wrappers, preferably Orientex

¾ cup [100 g] sliced jackfruit

Vegetable oil, for frying

TO MAKE THE SAUCE

In a small saucepan over medium heat, warm the coconut milk. Add the dark brown sugar and stir until dissolved. Cook the mixture, stirring frequently, until thick and jammy, about 25 minutes. Keep warm while you prepare the lumpia.

TO MAKE THE LUMPIA

1. Have a small bowl of water ready. Line a baking sheet with paper towels and set aside.

2. Spread out the light brown sugar on a plate. Roll the banana pieces in the sugar to coat.

3. Carefully separate the lumpia wrappers. To prevent them from drying out, cover the unused wrappers with a damp paper towel. Lay one wrapper on a clean work surface and place each sugar-coated banana near the edge closest to you. Top

with 1 Tbsp of the jackfruit. Roll up the edge toward the middle, then fold in both sides and continue rolling. Moisten the opposite edge of the wrapper with water to seal. Repeat with the remaining filling and wrappers.

4. In a large Dutch oven over medium heat, warm about 1 in [2.5 cm] of vegetable oil to 350°F [180°C]. Add the lumpia and fry until golden brown, 3 to 5 minutes, flipping once. When done, use a slotted spoon to transfer the lumpia to the prepared baking sheet. Serve immediately, with sauce on the side or spooned on top.

Leche Flan

✦ Flan is very popular in Mexico, which shares a border with California. Making it at home gives me a chance to travel south of the border in the kitchen. My leche flan needs an entire night to chill but only requires four ingredients. Travel with me, playas.

✦

SERVES 6 TO 8

½ cup [100 g] sugar

One 14 oz [400 ml] can sweetened condensed milk

1¼ cups [300 ml] evaporated milk

4 eggs

1. Preheat the oven to 350°F [180°C]. In a medium skillet over medium-low heat, add the sugar and cook, stirring constantly, until the sugar begins to melt. Lower the heat to low if the sugar begins to brown too quickly.

2. Once the melted sugar begins to turn a deep caramel color, about 12 minutes, carefully and quickly pour the syrup into a 8 in [20 cm] metal pie pan. Rotate the pan to allow the syrup to coat the sides and the entire bottom. Set the coated pie pan aside.

3. Combine the condensed milk, evaporated milk, and eggs in a blender and process until well blended, about 1 minute. Pour the mixture into the prepared pie pan and cover the pan loosely with aluminum foil.

4. Place the pie pan in a 9 by 13 in [23 by 33 cm] baking dish and carefully fill the baking dish with enough water to reach halfway up sides of the pie pan. Bake until the flan is set and a toothpick inserted in the center comes out clean, 60 to 65 minutes.

5. Remove the pie pan from the baking dish and let the flan cool in the pan for 1 hour. Cover the pan loosely with foil and refrigerate overnight.

6. To serve, run a knife around the edge of the pan to loosen the flan. Hold a serving plate tightly to the pan and invert. Carefully remove the pan from the flan, allowing the syrup to coat the top and pool around the sides of the flan. Serve.

INDEX

ISBN 978-1-7972-1371-2

Manufactured in China.

MIX
Paper from responsible sources
FSC™ C169962

DESIGN Vanessa Dina

ADDITIONAL WRITING
Sarah Billingsley, Kayla Stewart, Dena Rayess, Sandra Wu, Magnolia Molcan

MERRY JANE

10 9 8 7 6 5 4 3 2 1

Chronicle books and gifts are available at special quantity discounts to corporations, professional associations, literacy programs, and other organizations. For details and discount information, please contact our premiums department at corporatesales@chroniclebooks.com or at 1-800-759-0190.

Chronicle Books LLC
680 Second Street
San Francisco, California 94107
www.chroniclebooks.com